MW00945216

Springs In Dry Places

366 Short Thoughts For Thirsty Souls

by H. Lamar Smith

Happy 90th Birthday with appreciation
H. Lamar Smith
12-17-16

1

Springs In Dry Places

Copyright © 2016 by H. Lamar Smith.
Published as a Kindle book in 2016.
Published as a paperback book in 2016.

Other Books By H. Lamar Smith

Kindle and/or Paperback

In The Steps of The Shepherd

366 Short Thoughts for the Long Walk

The Disciples and The Teacher

366 Short Thoughts for Serious Disciples

Staying On The Way

366 Short Thoughts for 'Walking The Jesus' Way

Seasons for Deepening The Soul

134 Short Devotional Readings for your walk through Lent, Holy Week, the Seasons of Easter, and Seasons of Pentecost. There are 118 days outlined with 134 readings.

Permissions

Scripture quotations marked (NASB) are from the New American Standard Bible®, Copyright © 1960, 1962, 1963, 1968, 1971, 1972, 1973, 1975, 1977, 1995 by The Lockman Foundation Used by permission." (www.Lockman.org)

Scripture quotations marked (NIV) are from THE HOLY BIBLE, NEW INTERNATIONAL VERSION®, NIV® Copyright © 1973, 1978, 1984, 2011 by Biblica, Inc.™ Used by permission. All rights reserved worldwide.

Scripture quotations marked (ESV) are from the ESV® Bible (The Holy Bible, English Standard Version®), copyright © 2001 by Crossway, a publishing ministry of Good News Publishers. Used by permission. All rights reserved.

Scripture quotations marked (NRSV) are from the New Revised Standard Version Bible, copyright © 1989 National Council of the Churches of Christ in the United States of America. Used by permission. All rights reserved.

Scripture quotations marked (NKJV) are from the New King James Version®. Copyright © 1982 by Thomas Nelson. Used by permission. All rights reserved.

Scripture quotations marked (The Message) are from THE MESSAGE. Copyright © by Eugene H. Peterson 1993, 1994, 1995, 1996, 2000, 2001, 2002. Used by permission of Tyndale House Publishers, Inc.

Scripture quotations marked (KNT) are from The Kingdom New Testament: *A Contemporary Translation*. Copyright © 2011 by Nicholas Thomas Wright. HarperCollins Publishers. Used by permission. All rights reserved.

Dedication

To Lorri and Amy

My Sweet

Daughters-in-Law

Whose lives have
immeasurably enriched mine.

Contents

About the Author

H. Lamar Smith has served as senior pastor for 46 years, having pastored in Tennessee, Kentucky, Oklahoma and Alabama.

Trevecca Nazarene University is his Alma Mater from which he received both the B.A. and M.A degrees.

He has been a teacher of preachers, first in Nazarene Bible College Extension and later as teacher and Director of Alabama Nazarene School of Ministry. Many of his students have looked to him as mentor and confidant.

He is currently serving as Executive Assistant to the District Superintendent on the Alabama North District Church of the Nazarene.

He speaks in local churches for revivals, interim pulpit supply and Faith-Promise services. He speaks in workshops and in spiritual retreats for pastors.

He has three wonderful sons, six delightful grandchildren and two amazing daughters-in-law.

He enjoys writing, building, gardening and fishing.

Devotional Recommendations

"H. Lamar Smith's devotional thoughts come from a long ministry of preaching and teaching with a true shepherd's heart. He brings the essential truths of God's word in a powerful, succinct, and sometimes challenging way. Thank you for daily words of wisdom that are beneficial for a closer walk with Christ."

Charlotte Davis
Retired Teacher

***

"I always start my day with Brother Lamar's devotionals. While thoughtful and uplifting, they are plain-spoken and unflinching in their presentations of the Bible's truths. This is a refreshing rarity in our day of "feel-good" religion."

Danner L. House
Retired Teacher
Valley, AL.

***

"H. Lamar Smith's devotional thoughts are profound, insightful, and scriptural. Written in a down to earth style that is easy to understand, they provide practical encouragement based on God's timeless truth."

Karen Lowry
Author and Editor,
Ocala, Florida

***

"Some teach the Bible as history, a perpetual looking back. Lamar relates it to our daily walk with keen insight."

James Spruill, Pastor
Jason Chapel Church of the Nazarene
Dickson, TN

***

"I was blessed have Lamar Smith as my pastor for nine-plus years. During that time, I learned and grew so much spiritually because of his intense knowledge of the scriptures. This book is more of the same. I am so thankful for his divinely inspired talent (gift) that has truly changed my life."

Janice Walters, RN, CMSRN, TL
Mobile, AL

"Every morning I wake up anxious to read the daily devotional thought from H. Lamar Smith. Lamar's writing is challenging, encouraging, and most importantly inspired by the Truth found in God's Word! Lamar brings the written word to life in such a way our spiritual walk can grow every day! One of the best daily devotional thoughts I have encountered! I love them!"

Howard Wilson
Pastor
Sheffield First Church of Nazarene

***

"Armed with knowledge and love of the Word, the author uses the pen of a 'ready writer' to skillfully arrange thoughts that challenge the reader to glean deeper meaning from scripture. Lamar's subtle sense of humor adds punch to his comments creating a smile on the face of the reader. "

Wanda J. King
Guest Services Representative
Vanderbilt University Medical Center

***

"Pastor Lamar provides what appears to be a short devotional for the reader to quickly digest.

However, because of his close walk with the Lord, he supplies you with a rich word that must be meditated on throughout the day. I encourage you to allow God's word to shape your life with Lamar's devotions as one of the tools."

Bruce W. Hudson
Pastor
Pleasant Grove Church of the Nazarene

***

"Inspirational and insightful devotional readings. Always gives me reasons to think more deeply and grow more richly in the Lord. It is with anticipation I turn to his works."

Karen Schiesz Dean-Maddox
Family Nurse Practitioner

Foreward

These devotional thoughts have come out of my own devotional life over the last several years. Many of these have been sent out as e-mails or included on social media sites. This book is in direct response to many of my readers who have asked that these devotional thoughts be published in book form for regular and repeated readings. I send these forth with my heart's desire that they may be a blessing and a means of grace to my regular readers and new readers alike.

The devotionals contained here are written with the intention that they be short and to the point. It is my hope that they will be a spring-board of meaning throughout your day. You can read each of them in about a minute, but I trust that they will be food for thought throughout your day.

May the Lord bless you in your walk with Him. None of us have arrived yet, but we are pilgrims on a great journey with our Shepherd who is leading the way and is The Way.

H. Lamar Smith

Note to Reader

Springs In Dry Places is sent to you with the prayer that these short thoughts would enable you to drink deeply from Jesus, the Fountain of Living Waters. "He changes a wilderness into a pool of water and a dry land into springs of water" Psalm 107:35 (NASB).

These 366 devotional thoughts can be used as a part of your daily devotionals or as touchstones for meditation. Feel free to share them with your friends.

You have permission to quote any of these individual devotional thoughts in social media or your other writings. When doing so you may use the following statement. "Quoted from *Springs In Dry Places* by H. Lamar Smith, Used by Permission."

Each reading has a month-date indication above the title for those who want to follow the calendar in their readings. When the Christian calendar does not conform to the month-date numbering here, and most years it will not, you can begin reading 4-9 on Palm Sunday and read through 6-18 then go back or forward to pick up the skipped readings.

You may subscribe for free daily devotional emails at: http://christourholyway.com

1-1
Springs In Dry Places
The doctor said, "Drink plenty of water. You do not want to get dehydrated." Water is so essential to our bodies. The Water of Life is so essential to our spirits. The deserts we transverse in life's journey make us cry out for water. We do not have to wait until we get out of the desert to find water. Our Lord has provided it to us wherever we are. He has given us an internal well of water (Jn 4:14). The water He gives us is His own Spirit. He is the *Spring* that goes with us through all of our dry places!

Jesus answered and said to her, "Everyone who drinks of this water will thirst again; but whoever drinks of the water that I will give him shall never thirst; but the water that I will give him will become in him a well of water springing up to eternal life." John 4:13-14 (NASB)

1-2
The Gift Of Life
Life is a precious gift. We do not choose it. It came to us out of the bonding of our parents. More than that, it comes to us as a gift from God. The fact that we exist at all is a gift laden with wealth. To see it is to prompt worship. Life is indeed precious, not to be wasted but invested, not to be despised but treasured. No matter what our circumstances are, we have great gifts. All life ultimately comes from our Father. Falling into His loving embrace gives us a purpose and a mission for life.

"Come, you children, listen to me; I will teach you the fear of the LORD. Who is the man who desires life and loves length of days that he may see good? Keep your tongue from evil and your lips from speaking deceit. Depart from evil and do good; Seek peace and pursue it." Psalm 34:11-14 (NASB)

1-3
Seeking God

In our emphasis on grace we sometimes make it only about God seeking us. The Scriptures implore us to seek God. Daniel said, "So I gave my attention to the Lord God to seek Him by prayer and supplications, with fasting, sackcloth and ashes" (Dan 9:3 NASB). We are never to stop seeking the One who never stops seeking us. He wants us to seek Him with our whole heart and soul. He promises that when we do, then we will find Him (Deut 4:39). This is to be the highest priority of our lives.

"And without faith it is impossible to please Him, for he who comes to God must believe that He is and that He is a rewarder of those who seek Him." Heb 11:6 (NASB)

1-4
A Fallen World

Sometimes it seems like this fallen world keeps falling. Yet, God is at work in it through those who follow the ways of the Kingdom. He has come to bring light through us to those who sit in darkness. We are salt to the earth, a preserving influence. When we have been with our Lord, we are prepared to be with the world as salt. We will not despair, because He has promised to triumph through us. We will not give up on people, because He did not give up on us.

"You are the salt of the earth; but if salt has lost its taste, how can its saltiness be restored? It is no longer good for anything, but is thrown out and trampled under foot." Matthew 5:13 (NRSV)

1-5
My Faults And Yours
Before you turn the searchlight on someone else, turn it on yourself. It is easy to rant about what someone else is doing and be blind to what we ourselves are doing. We gaze fully at the flaws of others while seeing our own faults only in our peripheral vision, if at all. Before we say a word about the behavior of someone else, what if we ask ourselves, "What am I doing that is like that?" At the point of this revelation we will be able to give prayerful grace to the other.

"But do you suppose this, O man, when you pass judgment on those who practice such things and do the same yourself, that you will escape the judgment of God?" Romans 2:3 (NASB)

1-6
Getting Out Of Holy Huddles
Jesus was criticized for "welcoming" and "eating with" sinners (Luke 15). He responds with the parables of the lost sheep, the lost coin, and the lost son. Jesus was saying that His actions of *welcoming* and *eating with* sinners was a calculated operation to seek and welcome the lost into the Kingdom. Sinners are more valuable than sheep or coins; they are lost children of

15

the Father. Discipleship is more than huddling in our Bible studies, it is to go live among sinners and value them as precious persons made in the image of our Father.

"Likewise, I say to you, there is joy in the presence of the angels of God over one sinner who repents." Luke 15:10 (NKJV)

1-7
The Breath Of God
"And the LORD God formed man of the dust of the ground, and breathed into his nostrils the breath of life; and man became a living soul" (Gen 2:7 KJV). We are dust, but more than dust. We belong to earth. Nevertheless, we belong to the God of Heaven and are made in His likeness. Jesus came down by incarnation to touch us with the life of Heaven. He has given us His Spirit, the Breath of God, which makes dust live and thrive. It is this Breath of God that makes us human.

"Breathe on me, breath of God; fill me with life anew, That I may love what Thou dost love, and do what Thou wouldst do.

"Breathe on me, breath of God; until my heart is pure, Until with Thee I will one will, to do and to endure.

"Breathe on me, breath of God, till I am wholly Thine, Until this earthly part of me glows with Thy fire divine.

"Breathe on me, breath of God; so shall I never die,
But live with Thee the perfect life of Thine eternity." -
Edwin Hatch

1-8
Restitution

The tax collector Zacchaeus declared that he would
make things right with his fellowman by giving half his
wealth to the poor and restoring fourfold anything
dishonestly gained. He was acting with a social
response to the good news of the Kingdom that Jesus
was announcing. Restitution was his manifestation of
repentance. The Kingdom of God includes restored
relationships with God, lived out as restored
relationships with other humans. Working on human
relationships, asking for forgiveness and seeking to
right wrongs is evidence of the Kingdom's presence.

And Zacchaeus stood, and said unto the Lord;
"Behold, Lord, the half of my goods I give to the poor;
and if I have taken anything from any man by false
accusation, I restore him fourfold." And Jesus said
unto him, "This day is salvation come to this house,
for so much as he also is a son of Abraham." Luke
19:8-9 (KJV)

1-9
Everyone's Work Matters

When we are called out by the King to follow Him, we
bring to His Kingdom the uniqueness of who we are.
God wants to work with each person in and through
their differences. Because of our uniqueness, we
bring something to the Kingdom that no one else
brings. Christ yokes Himself with us to do something

through us that no one else can do, and it will go undone if we do not work with Him to do it. What an honor it is to work with the Lord Himself.

"To one he gave five talents, to another, two, and to another, one, each according to his own ability; and he went on his journey." Matthew 25:15 (NASB)

1-10
Our Pain And God's Pain
The story of Hosea is about a man who lived out a parable in which he painfully participated. The one to whom he was married would not be faithful to him. This was what God was experiencing with unfaithful Israel. Having been rejected by one you love helps to understand the pain of God when we do not return His love. Our deepest pain may give us an insight into the hurt of God and bring us to a deeper relationship with Him. On the cross God's pain became visible. In the cross our pain finds relief.

"When Israel was a youth I loved him, And out of Egypt I called My son...I led them with cords of a man, with bonds of love, And I became to them as one who lifts the yoke from their jaws; And I bent down and fed them...So My people are bent on turning from Me." Hosea 11:1, 4, 7 (NASB)

1-11
Valuing Our New Place
The desert really makes us appreciate water. Hunger makes common food taste like a banquet. Hard work makes us know the value of money. Being released from a dungeon gives us a new appreciation for the

beauty of the earth. Having been freed from the prison of sin, we now know the value of freedom in Christ. Having come out of the darkness of death, we now treasure life and light. Having been washed from our filth, we now relish the joy of being cleansed. Having been an alien and stranger, we now know what it means to be included in the people of God.

"But now in Christ Jesus you who formerly were far off have been brought near by the blood of Christ. So then you are no longer strangers and aliens, but you are fellow citizens with the saints, and are of God's household." Ephesians 2:13, 19 (NASB)

1-12
The Rubber Meets The Road
Have you found a daily dying that is a daily living? Have you found a giving up of self that is a finding of self? Have you learned that embracing your cross is embracing your resurrection? This is all paradox. This is also the secret of the Christian life. It is not an abstract spirituality, but actions that are connected with the daily trials of our life which test us. We do not get to be spiritual in isolation from the problems of life. We learn true spirituality where the rubber meets the road.

"Not that I speak from want, for I have learned to be content in whatever circumstances I am. I know how to get along with humble means, and I also know how to live in prosperity; in any and every circumstance I have learned the secret of being filled and going hungry, both of having abundance and suffering need. I can do all things through Him who strengthens me." Philippians 4:11-13 (NASB)

1-13
To Use Or To Serve
We are in an age where people use other people for their own personal gratification. It is a sad commentary on the user. It thwarts growth, denies real character and destroys community. Other people are not here for us to use, but for us to serve. To value a person for whom they are, expecting nothing in return, is the basis for fulfillment. Nothing gives more meaning to life than to enjoy and delight in another who is made in the divine image, accepting them just as they are, and for whom they are.

"Each of you should learn to control his own body in a way that is holy and honorable, not in passionate lust like the heathen, who do not know God; and that in this matter no one should wrong his brother or take advantage of him. The Lord will punish men for all such sins, as we have already told you and warned you." 1 Thessalonians 4:4-6 (NIV)

1-14
The Way Of The Transgressors
The way of living in sin is not the best way nor is it the easy way. "The way of transgressors is hard" (Prov 13:15). When we go against God's plan for how to live, there is misery and disorder. It disrupts life the way it is supposed to be lived. The commandments and the teachings of Jesus are given to us in love so that we will avoid this hard way. The way to live is to get in the yoke with Jesus and live the way He instructed us. We will find that His yoke is easy and His burden is light. Jesus' way is the best way to live.

1-15
Holiness And Sexual Purity
Christians cannot expediently separate the purity of the soul from the purity of the body. Holiness involves being set apart in the total person, including spirit, soul and body. In a culture where sex is honored as the highest of pleasures, Christians must be vigilant in sexual purity if they would inherit the Kingdom (I Cor 6:9). When the body is given to God as a living sacrifice, it becomes our "spiritual service of worship" (Rom 12:1-2).

"For this is the will of God, your sanctification; that is, that you abstain from sexual immorality...For God has not called us for the purpose of impurity, but in sanctification."1 Thessalonians 4:3, 7 (NASB)

1-16
Wages Or Gift
"For the wages of sin is death, but the gift of God is eternal life in Christ Jesus our Lord" (Rom 6:23). This verse is a concluding contrast of two ways of living laid out in the whole chapter. The verse contrasts *wages* and *gift,* earnings and grace. To live our lives in the pursuit of sin has a payoff of death. The opposite of death is *eternal life* for those *in Christ*. In the writings of Paul, *in Christ* is about living our lives in full solidarity with Christ. It is to trust our lives completely to Him. To follow Him in this kind of solidarity is to have the *free gift* of the life *of the age to come* that comes through the Son.

"The wages paid by sin, you see, are death; but God's free gift is the life of the age to come in the Messiah, Jesus our Lord" (Rom 6:23 KNT).

1-17

Lived-out Spirituality

It is not possible for the vast majority of believers to live in a cloistered spirituality in a lonely desert place. It is possible to live the routines of your daily life in connection with the Presence of the Lord. It is possible to live a life set apart to Him on your job, even while you are living it in an increasing secular culture. This can be done by praying without ceasing, rejoicing evermore and giving thanks in all things (I Thess 5:16-18). It can be done by constant dependence on Him and serving Him in all we do.

"Whatever you do, do your work heartily, as for the Lord rather than for men" Colossians 3:23 (NASB)

1-18

Living Our Devotion

Personal spirituality is vain if we are not seeking to advance the kingdom in acts of righteousness. Our piety is useless if it is not joined to deeds of compassion. Our faith without works is dead. Our devotional life is meant to equip us to live a life of devotion and service. It is not an end within itself. It is meant to equip us to be true disciples who follow our Mentor in all the ways He has taught us. It prepares us to get our hands dirty while keeping our hearts pure.

"Religion that is pure and undefiled before God, the Father, is this: to care for orphans and widows in their distress, and to keep oneself unstained by the world." James 1:27 (NRSV)

1-19

One World Government

We are headed for a global government. "The government shall be on His shoulders" (Isa 9:6). Jesus is called "King of kings and Lord of lords" (Rev 19:16). This is more than spiritual, it is political. "Every knee shall bow" is more than sanctuary worship. It is the acclamation that the government is out of the hands of presidents, kings, and governors and is now in the hands of the Lord. The kingdom has come. It is here. It will come fully on that great day when He comes. Praise be to God!

"I charge you...that you keep the commandment without stain or reproach until the appearing of our Lord Jesus Christ, which He will bring about at the proper time—He who is the blessed and only Sovereign, the King of kings and Lord of lords...To Him be honor and eternal dominion! Amen." 1 Timothy 6:13-16b (NASB)

1-20

When God Has Not Spoken

It is dangerous to speak for God when He has not spoken. To offer prophetic words that do not come to pass have shattered the faith of many. We have all observed the person that is too quick with "a word from the Lord." God keeps his own words but is not bound to honor the words others put in His mouth. God will judge all who speak for Him when He has not spoken. In worshipful humility, treasure the precious word of God as the holy thing it is.

"I have not sent these prophets, yet they ran: I have not spoken to them, yet they prophesied." Jeremiah 23:21 (KJV)

1-21
Others Oriented

God is focused on the other. The members of the Trinity thrive as a community of self-giving love. It is the nature of God to reach out to others in love. God is a fountain of love from which love pours. This love is focused on the other and is truly self-giving love. If this kind of love is in us, it will constantly flow away from us toward others. It must not be given for what we can get in return. It must not even be given so that it can be acclaimed as love. Any feeble expression of love we express pales in the face of His great love for us.

"But I will sing of your might; I will sing aloud of your steadfast love in the morning. For you have been a fortress for me and a refuge in the day of my distress. O my strength, I will sing praises to you, for you, O God, are my fortress, the God who shows me steadfast love." Psalm 59:16-17 (NRSV)

1-22
The Unity Of God's People

We are spiritually kin to all those who claim God as Father. We belong to all of those who follow Jesus. We are linked to them and they to us. We are brothers and sisters in a common family. When brothers and sisters turn on one another it breaks the heart of the Father. To disown other Christians is to cause pain to the Lord of all Christians. The Holy

Spirit is a uniting presence in the body of believers, and to divide from one another is to grieve the Spirit. Cherish your brothers and sisters. It makes God happy.

"May the God who gives endurance and encouragement give you a spirit of unity among yourselves as you follow Christ Jesus, so that with one heart and mouth you may glorify the God and Father of our Lord Jesus Christ. Accept one another, then, just as Christ accepted you, in order to bring praise to God." Romans 15:5-7 (NIV)

1-23
Outsiders Become Insiders
There were those who looked in and felt left out. Those inside would not give them a place at the table. They were treated like aliens and strangers. Then the accepting Jesus came along and loved them. His compassion saw them as sheep without a shepherd. He touched outcasts, lepers and those the establishment called unclean. His Jubilee kingdom forgave their sins and canceled their debts. They thronged Him, longing to touch Him. The King opened wide the doors and brought the outsiders inside to the banquet table.

Jesus said to them, "Truly I say to you that the tax collectors and prostitutes will get into the kingdom of God before you" (Matt 21:31b NASB).

1-24

Insiders Become Outsiders

There are those who think they are in who are out. They think they will be welcomed on the great day into the kingdom, but will find themselves on the outside, because they did not welcome sinners into the kingdom. They kept and guarded it for themselves. This displeased the King. They did not serve in the way He commanded. This is the way insiders will wind up being on the outside. May we be warned! It takes more to be *in* than to claim you are *in*. The real mark of being in is to reflect Jesus' kingdom hospitality toward the outsider.

"I say to you that many will come from east and west, and recline at the table with Abraham, Isaac and Jacob in the kingdom of heaven; but the sons of the kingdom will be cast out into the outer darkness; in that place there will be weeping and gnashing of teeth." Matthew 8:11-12 (NASB)

1-25

A Cleansing Walk

There is a cleansing from sin by confession (I Jn 1:9). There is also a daily cleansing that comes by walking in the light (I Jn 1:7). Walking in the Light is nothing less than a disciple following Jesus the Light. This is walking in obedience to our Lord. Such a disciple does not rest in an initial confession, but has chosen the path of discipleship as a serious follower of Jesus. The result of this relationship is cleansing. Walking in obedience with Jesus is walking with our Jubilee, sins forgiven and debts paid.

"If we say that we have fellowship with Him and yet walk in the darkness, we lie and do not practice the truth; but if we walk in the Light as He Himself is in the Light, we have fellowship with one another, and the blood of Jesus His Son cleanses us from all sin." 1 John 1:6-7 (NASB)

1-26
Lost Sheep

If there is saved, there is unsaved. If there is found, there is lost. If there is a coming to hope, there are some still left in despair. To be brought to the inside means there are those still on the outside. C. S. Lewis said, "Whatever it means to be on the outside, you do not want to be on the outside." All do not come to follow Christ. Some follow their own way. All roads do not lead home. There is a path that leads to destruction. There are lost sheep that need to be sought and returned to the fold.

"What man among you, if he has a hundred sheep and has lost one of them, does not leave the ninety-nine in the open pasture and go after the one which is lost until he finds it?" Luke 15:4 (NASB)

1-27
Touched By Heaven

Jesus came by incarnation as Emmanuel to restore His creation and creatures with the life of Heaven. After He ascended, He gave the baptismal pouring of His Spirit at Pentecost (Acts 2:4, 33). This means that we have available to us the very Spirit of the One who came from Heaven. We need the constant refillings of the life of Heaven with which to touch the world.

We are not ready to rightly touch this world until we have been touched by the Heavenly Dove.

"And when they had prayed, the place where they had gathered together was shaken, and they were all filled with the Holy Spirit and began to speak the word of God with boldness." Acts 4:31 (NASB)

1-28
Confess The Gap
If you always get it right, then there in nothing from which you ever need to repent. If you never make any mistakes, then there is nothing to confess. There is then no need for you to pray, "Forgive us our trespasses as we forgive those who trespass against us." Our failure to confess and repent is a sign of our entrenched self-righteousness. The biggest thing we need to confess is our failure to love. Sin, at its core, is a failure to love, the violation of the Great Commandment. Look at the love of Jesus, look at your love and then confess the gap.

Lord Jesus, when we see the great love You have for us and all people, and how self-sacrificial Your life was, and how You loved and forgave Your enemies while they were mistreating and crucifying You, and in all of this "You opened not your mouth" in protest, we confess that we have a way to go, until we are fully formed in Your likeness. Amen!

1-29
Christian Character
The character of the true Christian is the great evangelistic tool for advancing the Kingdom of God.

The character that pours its life out in service wins over God's enemies. We are to be people who serve because Christ has served us. We are to lighten loads, go the second mile, "cheer the faint and lift up the fallen". The world is hungry to see real Christians that live it 24/7/365. Authenticity draws! Genuineness is winsome! They are tired of our arguments for the validity of the faith and are starving for good examples. Lord, help us be that!

"Follow my example, as I follow the example of Christ." 1 Cor 11:1 (NIV)

1-30
The Self Revelation Of God
God has shown us what He is like in Jesus of Nazareth. Jesus said, "If you have seen me, you have seen the Father" (Jn 14:9). If you really want to get to know the Father, then gaze long and hard at Jesus. Not only gaze at Him, walk with Him, and you will know what it is to walk with the Father. Do the deeds of Jesus and you will sense the Father is near. Read about Him in the Gospels. Meditate on Him. Talk to Him in prayer. Be alone with Him. Be quiet before Him. You will then know your Father.

1-31
Knowing Yourself
Know yourself. Stop and look at your actions and reactions. Think about what makes you tick. There is a sense in which you do not fully know yourself. You need to ask God to reveal you to yourself so that you can bring who you are to the healing grace of God and become more of what you were meant to be in

Christ. The Holy Spirit is the great revealer of the human heart and the great revealer of God. Come to Him and let Him shape you. The Christian life is about renewal and transformation of the Christ follower.

"For to us God revealed them through the Spirit; for the Spirit searches all things, even the depths of God. For who among men knows the thoughts of a man except the spirit of the man which is in him? Even so the thoughts of God no one knows except the Spirit of God." 1 Corinthians 2:10-11 (NASB)

2-1
Doing Righteousness And Justice
Abraham was chosen to be the father of many nations. His works and faith are a model to be followed. We too are children of Abraham. His descendants are not merely people of faith; they are those who live out His legacy by doing righteousness and justice. Righteousness involves living right before God and putting to right things in and around us. Justice comes to the aid of those who are beaten up by abusive powers. Doing righteousness and justice is as much our devotion to the Lord as our quiet times.

"For I have chosen him, so that he may command his children and his household after him to keep the way of the LORD by doing righteousness and justice, so that the LORD may bring upon Abraham what He has spoken about him." Genesis 18:19 (NASB)

2-2
A Time For Laughter

Sarah laughed at the absurdity of an old woman having a baby. So did Abraham. Sometimes in our despair, answers look absurd. But remember, God can do what we cannot do. We are to trust Him for a way when it seems there is no way. The story of the Lord who can give a baby to a barren woman inspires us to hope. Fruitfulness is something that comes from God. The Lord brings possibilities out of impossibilities. Sometimes we just want to laugh at what God has done.

"Is anything too difficult for the LORD? At the appointed time I will return to you, at this time next year, and Sarah will have a son." Genesis 18:14 (NASB)

2-3
Speaking Enriching Words

Life is enriched when we speak words of grace to each other. Rich fellowship is based on more than presence. It is how we speak to one another. It is enriching speech and words that exhort which encourage and feed the spirit. "Let your speech be always with grace, seasoned with salt, that ye may know how ye ought to answer every man" (Col 4:6 KJV). Tender words create tender ties that bind us together. Be thoughtful and intentional with your words.

"Let no evil talk come out of your mouths, but only what is useful for building up, as there is need, so that your words may give grace to those who hear." Ephesians 4:29 (NRSV)

2-4

Non-Coercive Love

The love of God is not coercive. Love never forces its own way. We are free to respond, free to accept or reject. We can reject love, to the pain of God and to our own determent. We can receive it to ours and God's delight. "God is love", and His character of holy-love is behind all of His overtures toward us. Love is born in us when we fully embrace His great love for us. This unconditional love, when lived out to those in our lives in non-coercive ways, brings the God of love near to them.

"How often I have longed to gather your children together, as a hen gathers her chicks under her wings, but you were not willing!" Luke 13:34b (NIV)

2-5

Forgotten Places

The unnoticed places of the world often feel invisible to the rest of the world. They are thought of by people of power as unimportant. The poor that live there have little hope that anyone will come to their aid. But these unnoticed places are noticed by the God of the incarnation. He anxiously awaits those who will go at His bidding to these unnoticed places and proclaim that the Kingdom of God is near and then demonstrate it by pouring their lives out on the forgotten. The Lord of heaven and earth loses track of no place, nor the people who dwell there.

"And Jesus went about all the cities and villages, teaching in their synagogues, and preaching the gospel of the kingdom, and healing every sickness and every disease among the people." Matthew 9:35 (KJV)

2-6
Do Not Fear Dark Clouds
When we get on the topside of our dark clouds, we will find that they are fluffy white. On the top side the sun is still shining. When your storm is threatening you at its worst, remember the Lord is still for you. "But unto you that fear my name shall the Sun of righteousness arise with healing in his wings; and you shall go forth, and grow up as calves of the stall" (Mal 4:2). Remember that the Son of Righteousness is the Sun of Righteousness. He is the Light for your darkest night and your most cloudy day.

2-7
Envious words
Our words betray what is in our hearts. In a culture of consumerism, it is easy to fall into the trap of talking about how much we want. Envy is often accompanied by resentment for what another possesses. Envy thinks that, "I would be a better person to have that than they." Gratitude is stifled. Contentment is scolded. Spiritual blessings are seen as less valuable than material ones. Love for every person drives out envy. Scripture declares, "Love does not envy" (I Cor 13:4).

"Therefore, putting aside all malice and all deceit and hypocrisy and envy and all slander, like newborn babies, long for the pure milk of the word, so that by it you may grow in respect to salvation, if you have tasted the kindness of the Lord." 1 Peter 2:1-3 (NASB)

2-8
Sanctifying The Tragic
Relationships can bring great joy and great sorrow. Words, decisions and deeds of another can negatively affect all persons connected to them. To be affected by this means more than picking up the pieces and moving on. It means bringing your situation to the foot of the cross and to your Lord. Take a long look at the cross. There the Father sanctified the tragic and redeemed the world. The Father who did that for the Son can sanctify the tragedies of your life and bring redeeming things from it for your good and His glory.

"For he has graciously granted you the privilege not only of believing in Christ, but of suffering for him as well—since you are having the same struggle that you saw I had and now hear that I still have." Philippians 1:29-30 (NRSV)

2-9
Changing Your Default Settings
You make time to do what you want to do. You are becoming what you do. Habit! You are doing what you are becoming. Character! You are what you are doing. Habits shape character. Character changes habits. If you want your life to change, then it will be necessary to reset your default settings. This cannot be done by willpower alone. This must happen because you are drawing on God's grace to walk a new and better path.

"Who is wise and understanding among you? Let him show it by his good life, by deeds done in the humility that comes from wisdom." James 3:13 (NIV)

2-10
"Life Is Difficult"
In this world you will have trouble. "Life is difficult" is the opening line of M. Scott Peck's book, *The Road Less Traveled.* Jesus said, "In the world you have tribulation, but take courage; I have overcome the world" John 16:33b (NASB). His whole point is that you too can overcome. When things are bigger than you can handle, look at the model of Jesus. Draw on His grace, day by day and moment by moment.

2-11
Innocent About Evil
Paul, speaking as spiritual father, said to the church, "I want you to be wise about what is good, and innocent about what is evil" Romans 16:19b (NIV). "Innocent about evil" means not to experience it. Evil calls for persons to try it. Evil pleasure has the poison of death in it. We are better not to have ever experienced some things. The loss of innocence is not a pretty picture, and the consequences are great. If we will be "wise about what is good", we will avoid the degenerating experience of what is evil.

2-12
Ongoing Cleansing
As life unfolds, so does self-discovery. We keep learning things about ourselves, even after we have walked a long time with the Lord, that previously were

not at a conscious level.   When the light of God shines into the deep places of our heart and mind, discoveries about ourselves are made.   There is a need to bring these to a conscious level by recognition, confession and surrender for ongoing cleansing.   This is what builds the character of Christlikeness.   This is how the process of sanctification works.

Lord, keep me honest before you.   I remember yielding my all to you in total surrender. I want to be true to that by living it out everyday. Show myself to me. You know it better than I. Show me the roots of words and actions. Show me why I did this or that. I want my spirit to live in harmony with the Spirit of Christ.   When you show myself to me, may I never excuse or explain, but cry out for a deeper and deeper work in my soul.   Oh, Consuming Fire, run through me! Amen!

2-13
Your Life Rooted In His
He lives in us, therefore we live. He who conquered death has promised if we believe in Him, we will never die. We know we end up as dust. This is not cause for despair since we believe in the Living One who was raised from the dead. The Creator is our Savior, so death does not, and cannot, have the last word. He who made dust live by breathing into it the breath of life will make dust live again on that great resurrection morning.

Martha said to Him, "I know that he will rise again in the resurrection on the last day." Jesus said to her, "I am the resurrection and the life; he who believes in

Me will live even if he dies, and everyone who lives and believes in Me will never die. Do you believe this?" John 11:24-26 (NASB)

2-14
Identify With Your Father

The thing that guided Jesus through was His full identity with the Father. He was secure in the love of His Father. He trusted His Father through His suffering, His cruel death, and all the way into a sealed grave. I can enter my suffering for my Father. I can suffer rejection if I can just have His acceptance. I can lie down in my grave knowing that He can call me forth. I can be disgraced if I have His grace! I too can be secure in my Father's love.

"For this reason the Father loves Me, because I lay down My life so that I may take it again." John 10:17 (NASB)

2-15
Casting Crowns At His Feet

Pride loves crowns. Political leaders are reluctant to release their crowns. Religious leaders have sanctified theirs. Crowns show authority, position and attainment. We may want to think, "My crown is my own. I worked for it. I was elected to it. It is even because of my God-given gifts. It is certainly mine to wear." But the remarkable thing about the heavenly realm is that all crowns are cast at the feet of the worthy Lamb. If we are to live "on earth as in heaven" we must humbly declare ourselves unworthy of crowns.

"The twenty-four elders will fall down before Him who sits on the throne, and will worship Him who lives forever and ever, and will cast their crowns before the throne, saying, "Worthy are You, our Lord and our God, to receive glory and honor and power; for You created all things, and because of Your will they existed, and were created." Revelation 4:10-11 (NASB)

2-16
Glimpses Of Glory

Moses prayed, "Show me your glory" (Ex 33:18). He learns that seeing the face of the Lord and the fullness of His glory is something that humans cannot fully experience. Since God is so great, and we are so finite, He shows us Himself in glimpses of glory. We behold His glory in His Son (Jn 1:14). We do not see the glory as sightseers see a sight on their bucket list. It is life transforming! It reaches to the core of who we are. In seeing the glory we are transformed by the Spirit (I Cor 3:18). Seek the Lord, and let Him reveal what He will.

But He said, "You cannot see My face, for no man can see Me and live!" Then the LORD said, "Behold, there is a place by Me, and you shall stand there on the rock; and it will come about, while My glory is passing by, that I will put you in the cleft of the rock and cover you with My hand until I have passed by. Then I will take My hand away and you shall see My back, but My face shall not be seen." Exodus 33:20-23 (NASB)

2-17
Walking With Grief
Grief comes to us with the losses that occur in our lives. The loss of a spouse, a marriage, health, a job, and multiple other losses can plunge us into grief's pain. Grief does not come alone; it brings with it an array of emotions. We do not go around it; we go through it. We do not get over it; we learn to live with it. It is not easy. We survive by faith, and being empowered by grace, we can learn to thrive. When our props are gone, we learn to lean on the Lord.

Holy Father, help us to accept what we do not want. Help us to embrace a fresh brokenness and a new humility as we feel the pain of a fallen world. May we use it as an opportunity of fellowship with Jesus by feeling a bit of the pain He felt. Help us to know how to be there for our grieving friends. Amen!

2-18
Bless The Lord
I bless You, O Heavenly Father! Who am I to bless You? I am Your creature made in Your likeness. I am Your offspring. I am the child of Your care. I am the temple in which You dwell. I am a worshiper in Your courts. I am a servant in Your Kingdom. Though I am all of these and more, I bless You because of who You are. Sovereign King! Gracious Savior! Thoughtful Creator! Compassionate Master! Foundational Rock! Protecting Fortress! Mighty Defender! Faithful Shepherd! Unfailing Provider! May my sincere praise never fail to bless You!

"The LORD has established His throne in the heavens, and His sovereignty rules over all. Bless the LORD, you His angels, mighty in strength, who perform His word, obeying the voice of His word! Bless the LORD, all you His hosts, you who serve Him, doing His will. Bless the LORD, all you works of His, In all places of His dominion; bless the LORD, O my soul!" Psalm 103:19-22 (NASB)

2-19
Knowing God
Our God is holy, but approachable. He is exalted, but near. He is infinite, but intimate. Paul, in speaking of the *Unknown God*, said to those at Athens, "That they would seek God, if perhaps they might grope for Him and find Him, though He is not far from each one of us" (Acts 17:27). This fact is mind boggling. The God of the universe is near to "each one". Paul says that we are related to Him for, "We are His children." We are related for relationship. He desires nearness, companionship and partnership. What an awesome God!

2-20
Engage Or Escape
The gospel song said, "I cannot wait to leave this world of sin and sorrow!" We have heard a hundred variations of that escapism line. When Christ entered our space, He knew very well what awaited Him! He fully embraced a sinful world and its suffering. He stuck to it until He finished His work. That is our model! We have not embraced Him to escape the world and go off somewhere else. If we would be Christlike, we will not be trying to escape before our assignment is complete. We are to be fully engaged in our calling until He comes.

40

"That I may know Him and the power of His resurrection and the fellowship of His sufferings, being conformed to His death" (Philippians 3:10, NASB).

2-21
On Assignment

"I have glorified You on the earth. I have finished the work which You have given Me to do" John 17:4 (NKJV). Since we have been sent as Christ was sent, and since we are to be in the world as He was in the world (1 John 4:17b), we have a work to do which no one else can do. His work is all around us. We are present in the world to glorify our Father by our deeds, speech and manner of life. Our assignment is to carry out a servant ministry, which is like Him and for Him.

2-22
Four Life Changing Verbs

Trust! Delight! Commit! Rest! "Trust in the LORD. Delight yourself in the LORD. Commit your way to the LORD. Rest in the LORD." Trust the Lord completely with your situation. May your delight be in Him! Be delighted in the way He does things and in who He is. Enjoy the Lord! Commit! Turn it over to Him! Place it in His wisdom. And having done this, just rest in Him. Your life is in Good Hands. There is no need to fume and fret when we have learned to trust, delight, commit and rest.

"Trust in the LORD and do good; dwell in the land and cultivate faithfulness. Delight yourself in the LORD; and He will give you the desires of your heart.

Commit your way to the LORD, Trust also in Him, and He will do it. He will bring forth your righteousness as the light and your judgment as the noonday. Rest in the LORD and wait patiently for Him; do not fret because of him who prospers in his way, Because of the man who carries out wicked schemes." Psalm 37:3-7 (NASB)

2-23
Releasing Anger
"Cease from anger and forsake wrath; Do not fret; it leads only to evildoing" Psalm 37:8 (NASB). Our anger can seem so right because we see our cause and our way as being so right. Anger cries out for justice or to set the record straight. The more we hold to it, the more it holds to us. It poisons our thoughts. It tries to get us to set everything and everybody straight. There is a right anger and a wrong anger. Neither kind must be allowed to consume us.

2-24
Life's Brevity
"LORD,...Let me know how transient I am." Do you know yet how short your earthly days really are? A vapor! Wilting grass! A fading flower! A breath! A sigh! A blink of the eye! O Lord, teach us to not waste our time nor the gifts you have given us. We have today and this moment to do good, to serve and give ourselves to You by serving and giving ourselves to others. Help us not to fritter away this precious gift called life. Help us to glorify you all of our days. Amen!

"LORD, make me to know my end And what is the extent of my days; Let me know how transient I am. Behold, You have made my days as handbreadths, and my lifetime as nothing in Your sight; surely every man at his best is a mere breath." Psalm 39:4-5 (NASB)

2-25
Cease Striving
"Cease striving and know that I am God; I will be exalted among the nations, I will be exalted in the earth" Psalm 46:10 (NASB). We want to fix it! We fret when we cannot! We cannot be still. What we have to learn is to let go of things over which we have no control. But greater than that, we must know that He is God! When we give it to Him, He will be exalted. He will bring good out of bad and the helpful out of the hurtful.

2-26
Born To Love God
We are born to love God. This reality calls for obedience, service and worship. This is what it means to be human. Loving God gives us purpose. Without it we are adrift, trying to find things with which to fill the longing. This love for God is not a one way street. He loved us before we loved Him. While being His enemies, He died for us. The gift of His Son is an expression of that love. To realize His love for us drives our love for Him. This relationship is the foundation for the rest of life.

"We love him, because he first loved us." 1 John 4:19

2-27

The Faith Of Demons

Belief that does not express itself in works is not belief. Belief is also incompatible with resistance to the divine will. John Wesley said, "The devils believe and tremble, and are devils still." To claim belief while resisting the teachings of Jesus is unbelief. Resistance to Jesus' teaching puts us in the company of demons and not the saints. The marks of belief are obedience, walking in the light, and allowing your faith to work itself out as faithfulness to your Father.

"You believe that God is one. You do well; the demons also believe, and shudder. But are you willing to recognize, you foolish fellow, that faith without works is useless?" James 2:19-20 (NASB)

2-28

God Invests In You

The Father believes in you even when you do not believe in yourself. This belief is His grace. It is His action toward your healing. It is His commitment to enable your recovery and rehabilitation. It is the work of sanctification for your wholeness and spiritual health. He does believe in you. He is committed to you. He is on your side. He is not against you. "The LORD is for me; I will not fear" (Ps 118:6). "Who can be against me?" (Rom 8:31). To realize and embrace this is truly life transforming.

2-29

Holiness Is Relational

Holiness is derived from our relationship with God, who is holy. Holiness is not something we possess but a relationship into which we have entered. As a relationship it is ongoing. "Whatever touches the altar shall become holy" Ex 29:37 (ESV). Christ is our High Priest, Altar and Sacrifice. He does not give us a stock of holiness so we can say, "I got it." We are only holy in our relationship to Him. Relationships have to be maintained. If we have Him and He has us, then we are "In Christ," joined to Him. There is holiness in that union.

"The sin offering shall be slaughtered before the LORD at the spot where the burnt offering is slaughtered; it is most holy...Whatever touches its flesh shall become holy." Lev 6:25b, 27a (NRSV)

3-1
Job's Ashes And Jesus' Test
Jesus went into the wilderness to be tempted and tested by Satan. The test started there and did not stop until breath left His body on the cross. Job endured loss of family, property and health in his test. Jesus faced the forces of demonic powers, bore the weight of the sins of the world, and endured stripes that would heal others. There are times of testing for all God's children. If you are in the wilderness of trouble, look carefully and you will see the footprints of Jesus there.

"So Satan went out from the presence of the LORD, and inflicted loathsome sores on Job from the sole of his foot to the crown of his head. Job took a potsherd with which to scrape himself, and sat among the ashes." Job 2:7-8 (NRSV)

3-2

The Grace Of Endurance

Paul, in one of his prayers, speaks of the "God who gives endurance and encouragement" (Rom 15:5a). This is a wonderful statement, expressing one of the many facets of helping grace. By His Spirit God speaks encouragement to our minds and grants grace for endurance. This is a reminder that we are not alone. There is One with us who can refortify our souls with the encouragement of His Spirit. He will enable us to "endure hardship as a good soldier of Christ Jesus" (2 Tim 2:3).

3-3

Abused By Luxury

It is possible for children to be abused by luxury, never knowing the toil and struggles of labor. We are not on a life-long vacation, but a journey across the wilderness. The caterpillar that does not struggle to get out of the cocoon will never soar as a butterfly. To protect from struggle is a mistake. Unearned wealth is usually always squandered. Life without suffering seldom develops sympathy and empathy. Our Heavenly Father does not make His children immune to pain, suffering and difficulties. His future is prepared for the prepared.

"Consider it pure joy, my brothers, whenever you face trials of many kinds, because you know that the testing of your faith develops perseverance. Perseverance must finish its work so that you may be mature and complete, not lacking anything. James 1:2-4 (NIV)

3-4
Wilderness Complaints And Blessings
In real time, wilderness words sounded like these: "The food is bad". "Now Egypt, it really had some tasty food." "The sun is hot." "The desert is dry." "We left a good life for this?" After they came through the wilderness they said, "We had water to drink from a rock". "We had bread from heaven to eat". "Our shoes did not wear out." "Our God guided us by a pillar of cloud by day and a pillar of fire by night." "We inherited promises." We do not have enough perception to judge our lives by where we are at the moment. We must wait and see what God is birthing out of it.

"He spread out a cloud as a covering, and a fire to give light at night. They asked, and he brought them quail and satisfied them with the bread of heaven. He opened the rock, and water gushed out; like a river it flowed in the desert. For he remembered his holy promise given to his servant Abraham." Psalm 105:39-42 (NIV)

3-5
Learning How To Suffer
Suffering is not easy. It does help if we learn how to suffer. Without complaint! With patience! With perseverance! With humility! Like Jesus! Identify with all who have suffered before you. Identify with those around the world who even now experience greater sufferings than yours. Identify with the sufferings of your rejected Messiah. It is what joint-heirs do. It will bring a deeper acceptance of Him. Further, it becomes real knowledge of Him as you enter "the fellowship of His suffering" (Phil 3:10).

"And if children, then heirs; heirs of God, and joint-heirs with Christ; if so be that we suffer with him, that we may be also glorified together. For I reckon that the sufferings of this present time are not worthy to be compared with the glory which shall be revealed in us." Romans 8:17-18 (KJV)

3-6

Joseph's Season Of Lent

Joseph was the beloved son of Jacob's cherished wife, Rachel. He entered life celebrated. It looked like he might have been born with a silver spoon in his mouth, but he was destined for a life of suffering. Yes, he is going to save a nation in the end and play a key part in God's story, but first he must suffer. This is the part we do not like nor want. It is the way of the cross. Life has its sufferings woven together with its blessings. In this, God blesses others through our pain.

"As for you, you meant evil against me, but God meant it for good in order to bring about this present result, to preserve many people alive." Genesis 50:20 (NASB)

3-7

Rejected Saviors

Joseph's coat of many colors was a badge of honor given to him by his father. It was his father's celebration of a special son from barren Rachel. Joseph's brothers would not celebrate Joseph. They despised the one, who would be in time, their salvation. Jesus was the son of another Joseph who was a means of salvation to Israel and the world. He was rejected by those who should have embraced Him. The despised One became our Saving King!

"When they saw him from a distance and before he came close to them, they plotted against him to put him to death. They said to one another, "Here comes this dreamer! Now then, come and let us kill him and throw him into one of the pits; and we will say, 'A wild beast devoured him.' Then let us see what will become of his dreams!" Genesis 37:18-20 (NASB)

3-8
Rejection's Pain
Joseph's brothers rejected him out of jealousy. This rejection caused great pain to Joseph, and his presumed death was devastating to Joseph's father. A whole family mourned. Jacob lived a large part of his life in pain for his absent son. The brothers' failure to love Joseph, even in his immaturity, expressed itself as rejection. This rejection devastated a whole family. Another Father wept over the rejection of His Son and, in love, offered the rejected Son as Savior for all.

"So they took Joseph's tunic, killed a kid of the goats, and dipped the tunic in the blood. Then they sent the tunic of many colors, and they brought it to their father and said, "We have found this. Do you know whether it is your son's tunic or not?" And he recognized it and said, "It is my son's tunic. A wild beast has devoured him. Without doubt Joseph is torn to pieces." Then Jacob tore his clothes, put sackcloth on his waist, and mourned for his son many days." Genesis 37:31-34 (NKJV)

3-9
Refined By Fire
God turns bad things around to produce good. It may
be tragedy, sickness, pain and accidents. Given into
His hands, these are made to serve a greater
purpose. God by grace uses them to refine our
character. As Jesus "learned obedience through the
things He suffered," so our sufferings refine us to be
like Jesus. Gold and silver are refined by fire.
"Everyone will be salted with fire" (Mk 9:49). Holy
God, come to us as Refining Fire in the midst of our
tests.

3-10
Endurance
"If we endure, we will also reign with Him" (2 Tim
2:12a). By endurance, races are won, jobs are
completed and the Christian life is finished. Jesus
said about coming tribulation, "The one who endures
to the end, he will be saved (Mk 13:13, Mt 10:22,
24:13). We do not like endurance. It does not feel
comfortable. It is painful. It strains our muscles and
our faith. It strips us of our self-sufficiency. It makes
us pray. It moves us out of the comforts of the soft to
the company of the saints.

3-11
Humbled Before His Glory
The Lord is high and lifted up. He sits on His throne,
clothed in light and glorious majesty. The vision is so
glorious that in trembling we fall before Him. Who can
stand in His presence? One who still lives his or her
life in pride has never yet seen the enthroned glory of
the one exalted God. To see His glory is to see our

un-doneness. To see Him will take the swagger out of our step and cast us upon our face. "Our God is a consuming fire" (Deut 4:24). To see Him burns our pride and leaves us with a proper view of Him and consequently, a proper view of ourselves.

"Therefore, since we receive a kingdom which cannot be shaken, let us show gratitude, by which we may offer to God an acceptable service with reverence and awe; for our God is a consuming fire." Hebrews 12:28-29 (NASB)

3-12
Forgotten And Forsaken
Joseph was forgotten in prison. He was there because he refused to yield to the sin of adultery. He was there because a lie was told about Him. In spite of this, he thrived in prison. He was used of God even during this time of confinement. He shows kindness to fellow prisoners, but is forgotten. God did not forget him there, and God will not forget you there. When it looks like your life is on hold, your Father has not lost track of you.

"Yet the chief cupbearer did not remember Joseph, but forgot him." Genesis 40:23 (NASB)

3-13
Fire And Cloud
There was a pillar of fire by night that led the people across the wilderness. God's glory was hidden in a cloud by day, the same cloud that concealed Him on Mt. Sinai. At night the fire of His guiding presence burned the cloud back so the people could walk at

night.   Concealed and revealed!   Never far away! Always guiding!   Always with us!   With Him the wilderness does not consume us.   With Him we are refined to live in the promised land.

Lord, thank You for the wilderness that refines us to live in Canaan.   Thank You for trials that make us grateful for blessings.   Thank You for the tests that strip us of self-sufficiency and brings us to depend on You.

3-14
Dealing With Anxiety
"When my anxious thoughts multiply within me, Your consolations delight my soul" Psalm 94:19 (NASB). When we are confronted with stressful times and situations, the natural tendency is to feel anxious. Sometimes anxiety can be overwhelming.   We must not allow anxiety to have the final word.   In the midst of the stressful, we pray to the Lord for stamina.   We stand on His promises and find grace.   With the Spirit, we are ready to face our task and our life.   Look to Him, and turn anxiety into trust.

3-15
He Is With Us
Most of the time life does not wait for us to get ready when it throws problems our way.   We would like more time to assess the situation or even absorb the blow, but it is not an option.   Remember though, we do not have to muddle through when the Lord is with us.   He hears short desperate prayers for strength and wisdom. We hear Him say, "I will never leave you or forsake you" (Heb 13:5).   Our heart gives a

resounding, "Amen". He gives us His resources, and He always brings us through when we trust Him.

3-16
Energy Supply

Everywhere we look there are power cords and charge cords for this or that device. Everywhere we look in our lives there are charges of new energy that come to us from multiple sources. We get energy from friends and relationships. We get energy from learning and doing. We get energy by giving energy. Being with the creation gives us energy, as does art and beauty. We get energy from worship and sacrament. Our real source of energy is the Holy Spirit. He aids us in a thousand ways. He comes to us in real mystery with real energy for real renewal.

"Now may the God of hope fill you with all joy and peace in believing, so that you will abound in hope by the power of the Holy Spirit." Romans 15:13 (NASB)

3-17
Consuming Fire

We have watched with horror as raging forest fires have consumed everything in their path. The Israelites stood at the base of the mountain, and what was a cloud to Moses was seen as fire for them. It was both. Moses spent forty days there encountering the glory of God. Jesus came down to us to reveal the glory of His Father. To enter the cloud of glory is to experience the fire.

"When Moses went up on the mountain, the cloud covered it, and the glory of the LORD settled on

53

Mount Sinai. For six days the cloud covered the mountain, and on the seventh day the LORD called to Moses from within the cloud. To the Israelites the glory of the LORD looked like a consuming fire on top of the mountain. Then Moses entered the cloud as he went on up the mountain. And he stayed on the mountain forty days and forty nights." Exodus 24:15-18 (NIV)

3-18
The Unseen Hand
The hand that feeds us and supplies our needs is the hand of God. This Unseen Hand is here to lift loads, to strengthen, protect and defend. It works for us in ways we do not know. We know it is there, because we feel its motions and sense its touch. The Unseen Hand is shaping us like clay. It is working to make the best come out of the worst. Its presence gives us joy even in sorrow and hope when it seems there is no hope. Hold on to the hand that is holding you! All is well!

"We have thought on Your lovingkindness, O God, In the midst of Your temple. As is Your name, O God, So is Your praise to the ends of the earth; Your right hand is full of righteousness." Psalm 48:9-10 (NASB)

3-19
The Power Of Pity
As our Father has pity for His children so we are to have pity for each other. Pity is not a bad thing. The right kind of pity does not look down on another as pitiful. Pity is compassion that calculates the fragility of life. Our eyes tell the story. Look into the eyes of

another and you will often see a fragile soul. You may see abuse, pain, rejection, sorrow, grief, sadness, heartache, insecurity, loneliness and a vulnerable soul. Pity is love that senses another's vulnerability and seeks to give a healing touch.

"As a father pities his children, so the LORD pities those who fear Him. For He knows our frame; He remembers that we are dust." Psalm 103:13-14 (NKJV)

3-20
At Wits' End
They "were at their wits' end. Then they cried to the LORD in their trouble, And He brought them out of their distresses." The storm is great. The vessel is about to be swamped. No hope is in sight. You are at your wits' end. You have no answer for your plight. All you have tried has failed. You cry out to the Lord. Your prayers are desperate. The One who loves you comes to your aid and sees you through. He brings your little boat to a calm haven. You bow in worship.

"They reeled and staggered like a drunken man, and were at their wits' end. Then they cried to the LORD in their trouble, And He brought them out of their distresses. He caused the storm to be still, so that the waves of the sea were hushed. Then they were glad because they were quiet, So He guided them to their desired haven. Let them give thanks to the LORD for His lovingkindness, and for His wonders to the sons of men! Let them extol Him also in the congregation of the people, and praise Him at the seat of the elders." Psalm 107:27-32 (NASB)

3-21

A Very Present Help

We do not serve God to use Him for our benefit. However, without doubt, serving God means He is always present with us to help us. Sometimes His help is obvious. Sometimes it is not. He does a thousand things a day for us that we cannot see. He has our back. He is our defense on all sides. The One with us gives us strength, wisdom and a flowing stream of grace. Oh, worship your King. Give Him honor and praise!

"God is our refuge and strength, A very present help in trouble. Therefore we will not fear, though the earth should change and though the mountains slip into the heart of the sea; though its waters roar and foam, though the mountains quake at its swelling pride." Psalm 46:1-3 (NASB)

3-22

Dying For Sinners

Why would someone lay down their life for mean people? Sinners? Rebels? God haters? The Self-centered? The arrogant? Evil persons? The unkind, unthankful and the unruly? Just outright bad folks? One Man did it! Jesus! He did not rant about how bad the world was, nor how bad its people were. He just got busy giving up His life for them. It was the greatest action of love in human history! These are steps we follow!

"For one will hardly die for a righteous man; though perhaps for the good man someone would dare even to die. But God demonstrates His own love toward us, in that while we were yet sinners, Christ died for us." Romans 5:7-8 (NASB)

3-23
King Of The Earth
"Sing praises to our King, sing praises. For God is the King of all the earth" Psalm 47:6b-7a (NASB). God is King above all kings, Ruler above all rulers and LORD of all Lords. His kingdom is called the Kingdom of God. When churches, societies, governments, and individuals come under His sovereign rule, then justice and peace thrive. To demonstrably live under His kingship is the best witness we can make of our faith. It speaks louder than our words. May the way we live praise our King.

3-24
Free From Shame
God's gracious forgiveness releases us from guilt. The same grace also seeks to release us from shame. So many people carry shame from childhood abuse. Others carry it from some unthoughtful act they did at another time and place. Shame is a heavy burden to bear. You do not have to bear it alone. One bore it with you and for you. He who was crucified naked took upon Himself every shameful act of humanity. He not only bore your sins, He bore your shame. Receive this gift of grace.

"Fixing our eyes on Jesus, the author and perfecter of faith, who for the joy set before Him endured the cross, despising the shame, and has sat down at the right hand of the throne of God. For consider Him who has endured such hostility by sinners against

Himself, so that you will not grow weary and lose heart." Hebrews 12:2-3 (NASB)

3-25
The Beauty Of Unity
In a world of name calling, sectarianism, and petty differences, unity is fractured. The Father not only wants His church to live in unity, He wants all of His creation to dwell in unity. Instead of doing the things that make for peace, we do the things that insure division. We speak without thinking. We talk without listening. We pin labels on others so we can close our ears to their opinions. Christ came to unify all humanity around Himself and has charged us to be His ambassadors, reconcilers and peacemakers.

"Behold, how good and how pleasant it is for brothers to dwell together in unity! It is like the precious oil upon the head, coming down upon the beard, even Aaron's beard, coming down upon the edge of his robes. It is like the dew of Hermon coming down upon the mountains of Zion; For there the LORD commanded the blessing—life forever." Psalm 133:1-3 (NASB)

3-26
Getting Hurt By The Lord
"Peter was hurt because Jesus asked him the third time, 'Do you love me?'" John 21:17 (NIV). The hard questions can hurt. They force us to face what we do not want to face. They call on us to go further and deeper. They require that we express our love by service. Facing the questions that hurt can bring

healing. The Lord who has hurt us is the One who can heal us.

"Come, let us return to the LORD; for it is he who has torn, and he will heal us; he has struck down, and he will bind us up." Hosea 6:1 (NRSV)

3-27
He Is Mine
If you can say to God, "I am yours", then you can truly say, "He is mine". He receives our all so that He may give us His all. He asks us to release what is in our hand so He can give us what is in His hand. We release the lesser, and He gives us the better. He awaits the confession of our emptiness so He can give us His fullness. He awaits our surrender to give us victory.
"For of His fullness we have all received, and grace upon grace." John 1:16 (NASB)

3-28
"All Things Belong To You"
The Levites were not given a tribal portion in the land, because the Lord was their portion. How we crave a place that is our own! We spend a lifetime carving out a portion and staking our claims. If I know that the Lord is my portion, then I possess all things. I can then hold things loosely and hold Him firmly. To be in Christ is to inherit all things, knowing real wealth.

"All things belong to you, and you belong to Christ; and Christ belongs to God." 1 Corinthians 3:22-23 (NASB)

3-29
Internal Self-Abuse

It is easy to silently beat ourselves up over something we did or did not do. Behind this is perfectionism and self-righteousness. The belief that we should have acted perfectly in the past needs to be released. Know that you are a person that needs grace like everyone else. Christ has given you grace. Stop withholding it from yourself as if you are special and do not need it. Receive it and be thankful.

"And from Jesus Christ, the faithful witness, the firstborn of the dead, and the ruler of the kings of the earth. To Him who loves us and released us from our sins by His blood." Revelation 1:5 (NASB)

3-30
Joy In The Hidden Life

The life "hidden with Christ in God" cannot be about me. It cannot call attention to itself. It cannot exalt itself on a throne, because only One is worthy of the throne. It cannot be about accolades and honors. It can only be about humility, reverence and gratitude that I am one with Him. I rejoice when He is advanced, when He increases and I decrease, and when He is praised.

For you have died and your life is hidden with Christ in God. When Christ, who is our life, is revealed, then you also will be revealed with Him in glory." Colossians 3:1-4 (NASB)

3-31

In The Other's Place

Jesus gave us the Golden Rule. "As you would that others do unto you, do also to them." It is only possible to do this when we thoughtfully pause and put ourselves in the other person's place. It is not enough to say, "Well, I know what I would want done!" Sensitivity is required. Seek to feel the other person's situation, their culture and background. Listen to their story. Learn what has shaped them. Putting yourself in their place enables you to act with that person's best interest at heart.

4-1

Thoughts And Sin

Something goes awry in our thinking before sin becomes an action. We embrace a kind of rationale that says, "This is okay, not so bad, and will not hurt anything or anybody." This is why the renewal of the mind (Rom 12:2) and having the mind of Christ (Phil 2:5) is so important to keep away from even the hint of sin. We are admonished, "To abstain from the very appearance of evil." We also need to know that we are to abstain from the kind of thinking that leads to evil.

"For out of the heart come evil thoughts, murders, adulteries, fornications, thefts, false witness, slanders. These are the things which defile the man" Matthew 15:19-20a (NASB).

4-2

He Is Restoring

None of us have it all together. We all have things that are out of place, things that need restoring and things that need God's mercy. We are all needy people. We can be rich and yet impoverished. We can look whole and yet be broken. In humility, we must acknowledge our need for help. We must not judge others, but by the Spirit judge ourselves. He is very aware of where we are and where He is trying to take us. Let Him! He will!

"Hear, O LORD, and be gracious to me! O LORD, be my helper!" Psalm 30:10 (NRSV)

4-3
Fellow Travelers
When you see people stuck where you used to be, pray for them. Do not judge them. You matured past where they are, so be patient with them. The Lord who brought you out is bringing them out. Do not rush the process. Do not think green fruit will not ripen. Do not judge spotted fruit. Pray for them. Love them like someone loved you. Encourage them on the right road. Someday they may pass you. If they do, you will rejoice and be glad.

"My friends, if anyone is detected in a transgression, you who have received the Spirit should restore such a one in a spirit of gentleness." Galatians 6:1a (NRSV)

4-4
Changing Histories Changes History
We live in a world where so many people seem increasingly broken. Abuse, addictions, sinful behaviors, and corrupt thinking have them in chains, decay and repeated cycles of failure. God can break

these generational cycles. He can create new stories. He can give them hope and a fresh start. God can begin something transformational in their families, changing the outcome of their story and changing history.

Father, I am so grateful someone brought the good news of Jesus to us. It has forever changed my story and the story of my family. Lord, enable us to be loving witnesses and godly examples that can change another person's life story. And may we live our story in such a manner that it fits in Your larger story.

4-5
Letting God Restore Us
"Do you want to get well?" is what Jesus said to the man who had been in his condition for 38 years (John 5:6). This man had lost the will to be better. He had accepted his plight. Jesus is trying to stir something in his heart by His question. Jesus wants to release us from what holds us back. We must want what He wants for us. But more than that, we must have a Power enter our lives that is greater than the power of self-help or determination. Our restoration will be a God thing!

Lord, we have been a long time where we are. You have entered our lives to bring us to a new location. May we never get accustomed to where we are when You are calling us to a better place in You. Amen!

4-6
Spirit And Body
What we do with our body affects our spirit. To neglect the body is to neglect the spirit. Sins of the spirit also hurt our bodies. We poison our bodies by our attitudes. We are an undivided whole. In Christianity we are not a mere spirit that floats off somewhere else when we die; we will eventually be reunited with resurrected bodies in a healed wholeness to inhabit the new creation. Our Father will redeem us, spirit, soul and body!

Father, may we care for our bodies, since they are your temple, and Your Spirit lives in us. Cleanse our spirits from all that is not like Your Spirit. May we let Your Spirit live out of our bodies in incarnational ways, even as our Lord did. Amen!

4-7
Cultural Voices
The cultural voices seem to be saying, "If it feels right, it can not be wrong." The culture feeds on itself. If it says a thing is right, then more and more people go along with the combined voice, erasing moral qualms. History is full of wrecked lives of persons who did what they felt was right at the time. Whole nations have fallen in moral collapse. Racism, genocide, inquisitions, communal depravity, and other outrages have happened with full public approval. We need the moral code of Scripture. We need a standard that sits above us and judges us.

"And you shall have the tassel, that you may look upon it and remember all the commandments of the LORD and do them, and that you may not follow the harlotry to which your own heart and your own eyes are inclined." Num 15:39 (NKJV)

4-8
Follow Me
When Jesus called Peter and the others from their boats, He said to them, "Come, follow me, and I will make you fishers of men" Matthew 4:19. They followed him for an amazing 3 1/2 years. Then it ended. They went back to their nets. The resurrected Jesus came back to the sea shore to call them again. He says to Peter, "Follow Me" (John 21:19, 22). Now he sees that it means something deeper. Now it means, "feed my sheep and my lambs," followed by death on a cross. Jesus is unrelenting with the command, "Follow Me."

4-9
A Kingdom Portrait
Palm Sunday was the day that Jesus publicly presented himself as Israel's Messiah by acting out an OT prophecy. He even paraded the kind of humble Kingdom He was bringing. Look at the man on the donkey! He does not look like the promised descendant of David! He does not look like one whose dominion will be from "sea to sea" and "to the ends of the earth!" But, you just wait and see! His Kingdom marches on! The rejoicing on Palm Sunday anticipates the day when all will shout, "Blessed is he who comes in the name of the Lord" (Ps 118:26, Mt 21:9, Lk 13:35).

"Rejoice greatly, O daughter of Zion! Shout in triumph, O daughter of Jerusalem! Behold, your king is coming to you; He is just and endowed with salvation, Humble, and mounted on a donkey, Even on a colt, the foal of a donkey...And He will speak peace to the nations; And His dominion will be from sea to sea, And from the River to the ends of the earth" Zechariah 9:9-10.

4-10
Glory And Cross

The cross is the crown and the glory. We do not think of it that way. We think the glory comes in the parade after the victory is won, then you wear the crown. Jesus referred to the cross as His glorification. He wore the crown of thorns in agony. Jesus by "the suffering of death was crowned with glory," and He "brings many sons to glory" (Heb 2:9-10). Saints through the ages have revealed the glory of God, even in their sometimes horrific deaths.

Therefore when he had gone out, Jesus *said, "Now is the Son of Man glorified, and God is glorified in Him; if God is glorified in Him, God will also glorify Him in Himself, and will glorify Him immediately." John 13:31-32 (NASB)

4-11
Thorns And Suffering

Between Eden and New Creation, we still deal with thorns and suffering. It was no accident that our Lord wore a crown of thorns. The Eternal Son came into a world of suffering, both to express His solidarity with the suffering and to lay the foundation for the full restoration of all things. Meanwhile, there are still thorns and all kinds of suffering that afflict us. He suffered with us; now we suffer with Him. To suffer with another is to know the most intimate of human bonds. So it is when we suffer with our Lord.

They stripped Him and put a scarlet robe on Him. And after twisting together a crown of thorns, they put it on His head, and a reed in His right hand; and they knelt down before Him and mocked Him, saying, "Hail, King of the Jews!" Matthew 27:28-29 (NASB)

4-12
Jesus' Treatment of Judas
If you have a Judas, treat him as Jesus did. Wash his feet. Give him the sop at the meal, something reserved for the honored guest. Treat him kindly. Make sure that you have love for the person. Love him until the end. Know your love can be rejected. Know that even demonic powers can be involved. Still love. Accept the betrayal. Commit the whole thing to your Father. Do not let it embitter your spirit. Do not let it turn you from your mission. In Jesus' sweetness, let it go.

Jesus answered, "It is the one to whom I will give this piece of bread when I have dipped it in the dish." Then, dipping the piece of bread, he gave it to Judas Iscariot, son of Simon. As soon as Judas took the bread, Satan entered into him. "What you are about to do, do quickly," Jesus told him. John 13:26-27 (NIV)

4-13
Tasting Death For All
On the cross, Jesus suffered death for everyone. When the Word was made flesh, it was destined to

die.   This is one of the places incarnation was headed. "He humbled Himself and became obedient to death, even death on a cross" (Phil 2:8).   Jesus "tasted death for everyone" as a gift of God's marvelous grace.   He tasted our death so we can taste His life. He died with us, and we die with Him. We die with Him that we might rise with Him.

"But we see Jesus, who was made a little lower than the angels, for the suffering of death crowned with glory and honor, that He, by the grace of God, might taste death for everyone." Hebrews 2:9 (NKJV)

4-14
Christ On The Cross
Death sentence. Executioners act. A Roman cross. Stop. Pause. Look. Listen. Feel. Smell. Blood pours. Flies swarm. Thorns throb. Jesus forgives. Vinegar offered. Politicians gloat. Friends forsake. Crowd rails. Men gaze. The hardened laugh. Religionists delight. Demons taunt. Women weep. Soldiers gamble. Disciples scatter. Breath departs. The Lamb dies. Sword pierces. Rome is relieved. The earth quakes. The sun hides. God weeps. Veil is torn. It is finished. Sacrifice completed. Death is defeated. Serpent is crushed. Love wins.

Therefore when Jesus had received the sour wine, He said, "It is finished!" And He bowed His head and gave up His spirit. John 19:30 (NASB)

4-15
Holy Saturday Remorse

O Suffering Servant, we could not watch with You for one hour. We left You alone in Your pain. We slept while You prayed. Your soul was in deep anguish. We needed our rest. Forgive us! We had not yet discovered suffering love. We forgot we were partners with You in this mission of hurting with the hurting. We had not learned the triumph of redemptive suffering. Even now, we want Your cross to be our salvation, but we shrink from the cross being a way of life. Watching with You enables us to triumph in our temptations. Amen!

Then He *said to them, "My soul is deeply grieved, to the point of death; remain here and keep watch with Me." And He went a little beyond them, and fell on His face and prayed, saying, "My Father, if it is possible, let this cup pass from Me; yet not as I will, but as You will." And He *came to the disciples and *found them sleeping, and *said to Peter, "So, you men could not keep watch with Me for one hour? "Keep watching and praying that you may not enter into temptation; the spirit is willing, but the flesh is weak." Mt 26:38-41 (NASB)

4-16
The Resurrection Answer

The Resurrection of Jesus answered the Psalmist when he asked, "Will the departed spirits rise and praise You?" Jesus provided a living example of Resurrection when His Father raised Him from the dead. Jesus is our true hope over death. His resurrected-new-creation body foreshadows the body we will have. In our Messiah, death does not have

69

the final word, life does. Yes, the departed will rise to praise Him.

"Will You perform wonders for the dead? Will the departed spirits rise and praise You? Will Your lovingkindness be declared in the grave? Your faithfulness in Abaddon? Will Your wonders be made known in the darkness? And Your righteousness in the land of forgetfulness?" Psalm 88:10-12 (NASB)

4-17
Facing Death Without Fear
Face death with fear or face it standing in Christ's empty tomb. Look at Him in the tomb. Look at yourself there with Him. Look at Him coming out of the tomb and you following right behind Him. That is what it means when it says, "He was the first fruits from the dead." By His death He trampled down death. With His power He rendered death's pull powerless to those who are in Christ. In His triumph is our triumph. In his victory, we are victorious. By His life, we are raised to eternal life!
"But Christ has indeed been raised from the dead, the first fruits of those who have fallen asleep." 1 Corinthians 15:20 (NIV)

4-18
Resurrected Over Hate
If we must have someone to despise or hate, it should reveal to us that we are not yet like our Lord. Hate belongs to another kingdom. Hate belongs to the realm of death. Jesus triumphed over hate. His resurrection proves it. When we are risen from the dead with Him, we will seek those things which are

70

above. We will live by the higher. We will live by love, which triumphs over hate. If He "lives within my heart," then love is enthroned there.

"If then you were raised with Christ, seek those things which are above, where Christ is, sitting at the right hand of God. Set your mind on things above, not on things on the earth. For you died, and your life is hidden with Christ in God." Col 3:1-3 (NKJV)

4-19
Old Master Or New Master
Jesus did not come to rescue us in our sins but from our sins. He did not come to give us a blank check or an indulgence for a night with our old master. He came to break the chains that bind. He came to break the dominion and domination of sin in our lives. He came to bring us into "the glorious liberty of the children of God," no longer slaves, but sons and daughters of the King. In Him, the power of grace is greater than the power of sin. Know that grace is much more than mercy or unmerited favor; it is enabling power over sin's predominance.

"Even so consider yourselves to be dead to sin, but alive to God in Christ Jesus. Therefore do not let sin reign in your mortal body so that you obey its lusts, and do not go on presenting the members of your body to sin as instruments of unrighteousness; but present yourselves to God as those alive from the dead, and your members as instruments of righteousness to God. For sin shall not be master over you, for you are not under law but under grace." Rom 6:11-14 (NASB)

4-20

Old Life Or New Life

The resurrection of Jesus demonstrates that we are released from our old master, sin. The New Master has come. The old master of sin pays off with wages of death. The New Master pays off by sharing His life. The old life was driven by passion for sinning. The new life is driven by the passion of loving God with our whole being. The old life was about presenting ourselves to sin as our worshipful master. The new life is about presenting ourselves to God as slaves of righteousness, resulting in sanctification, and the outcome is eternal life (Rom 6:13, 19, 22).

"Therefore we have been buried with Him through baptism into death, so that as Christ was raised from the dead through the glory of the Father, so we too might walk in newness of life. For if we have become united with Him in the likeness of His death, certainly we shall also be in the likeness of His resurrection, knowing this, that our old self was crucified with Him, in order that our body of sin might be done away with, so that we would no longer be slaves to sin; for he who has died is freed from sin." Rom 6:4-7 (NASB)

4-21

Risen To Love

The resurrection of Jesus from the dead was more than the triumph of life over death. It was also the triumph of love over hate. If we have been risen with Him, we have been raised to a life of Jesus' kind of love. Love reigning in our hearts expels hostility and hate. Because Christ is risen in us, non-love things can no longer have the throne. Our words and actions testify to what reigns in us. It is our witness. We have been risen to love.

"If then you have been raised with Christ, seek the things that are above, where Christ is, seated at the right hand of God." Colossians 3:1 (ESV)

4-22
He Wants Your Love
When Jesus asked Peter, "Do you love me?" (John 21:17), He did not do it out of His own insecurity. It matters to Him if we love Him, because it is so important to our well being. Love is not a touchy-feely something. It is not a mere emotion. It is to feed sheep and follow Him. Love is a practice. Love demonstrates itself by service and keeping Jesus' commands. He is asking us today, "Do you love me?"

"If you love Me, you will keep My commandments." John 14:15

4-23
Death's Time
Sometimes we know by prognosis or diagnosis that our death is near. A few know by intuition. For the vast majority, we do not know. It comes as a surprise, unannounced. Death comes in the midst of jobs partially done and dreams not yet fulfilled. It interrupts and disrupts our lives. We really know it is coming, but do not expect it now. The announcement of death's destruction was made by the resurrection of the Son of God. The Life of God in us is the assurance that death does not have the final say. In

Christ, we are destined for resurrection and new creation glory.

"Behold, I tell you a mystery; we will not all sleep, but we will all be changed, in a moment, in the twinkling of an eye, at the last trumpet; for the trumpet will sound, and the dead will be raised imperishable, and we will be changed. For this perishable must put on the imperishable, and this mortal must put on immortality. But when this perishable will have put on the imperishable, and this mortal will have put on immortality, then will come about the saying that is written, "Death is swallowed up in victory. O death, where is your victory? O death, where is your sting?" 1 Corinthians 15:51-55 (NASB)

4-24
Evangelizing
We have our plans of salvation that can make people feel manipulated and produce phony converts. If we would live the compassion of Christ, stop trying to change people and love them for what they are, through His Spirit in us, we could be true evangelists. To live the principles of the kingdom of kindness, accepting love, lowly servanthood, and active compassion, would cause people to run over us to get into this Kingdom and follow this Lord. Jesus truly loved sinners, and they were drawn to Him by the sheer force of His love and His message. If it worked for Him, it will work for us.

Jesus said, "Go and make disciples" Matt 28:19

4-25
Measuring Wealth

Pity the person who measures wealth only by money and possessions. We will never come into a full rest of soul until we are freed from our inordinate drive for a better bottom line. We need to discover that true wealth is more than what we can hold in our hands. It is holding those we love in our heart. It is to discover the riches God has placed all around us in His glorious creation. It is to walk a path that celebrates intangible gifts. It is to find treasure each and every day in places the children of this world miss. No one is poor who has God as his Father.

"Then the Almighty will be your gold and choice silver to you. For then you will delight in the Almighty and lift up your face to God." Job 22:25-26 (NASB)

4-26
Being Real

Being two persons is not real. Being someone else is not real. The essence of not being real is to have a divided heart. To unite the whole person around God by driving out all idols is to unite the personality and to become real. This is the core of sincerity. To live in humility before God is reality. It is to be real. To live in pride and arrogance is false reality. Being real is the great need of every Christian. When it does not happen, it is a turn-off. When it happens, it is winsome evangelism.

"Teach me Your way, O LORD; I will walk in Your truth; Unite my heart to fear Your name. I will give thanks to You, O Lord my God, with all my heart, And will glorify Your name forever." Psalm 86:11-12 (NASB)

75

4-27

Tending Toward Forgiveness

Lasting relationships, more often than not, have an unspoken lean toward forgiveness. Forgiveness means that we forgo justice, when offended, for the greater benefit of the relationship. There can be a climate that, when there is an offense, it is not picked up by demanding justice. This is also a form of forgiveness. Jesus said, in the midst of injustice, and without being asked, "Father forgive them." He died for transgressors while they were transgressing. Forgiveness is a form of death to self. God's lean toward mercy is the grace that saves us.

"But God, being rich in mercy, because of His great love with which He loved us, even when we were dead in our transgressions, made us alive together with Christ (by grace you have been saved)." Eph 2:4-5 (NASB)

4-28

A Call To Discipleship

Conversion is more than being brought into a propositional decision; it is to hear the call of Christ and to follow as His dedicated disciple. Our plans of salvation have misunderstood the gospel and made discipleship and holiness unnecessary. Jesus calls us to be saved by losing our life. He calls us to die to live. He calls us to a cross. Following Him changes our world view, our value system and our total manner of living. Following Jesus will make us walk in a different manner than the prevailing culture.

And He summoned the crowd with His disciples, and said to them, "If anyone wishes to come after Me, he

76

must deny himself, and take up his cross and follow Me. For whoever wishes to save his life will lose it, but whoever loses his life for My sake and the gospel's will save it." Mark 8:34-35 (NASB)

4-29
Stars In The Night
A dark world needs light. The *Sun of Righteousness* has sent us out as stars in the dark. He said, "You are the light of the world" (Mt 5:14). Daniel reminds us, "Those who are wise shall shine like the brightness of the sky, and those who lead many to righteousness, like the stars forever and ever" Dan 12:3 (NRSV). Paul reminds us that by living moral and ethical lives, being blameless and innocent children of God without complaining or arguing, is to be a light to a "crooked and perverse generation." Let your life be a guiding star in a dark place.

"Do all things without murmuring and arguing, so that you may be blameless and innocent, children of God without blemish in the midst of a crooked and perverse generation, in which you shine like stars in the world." Phil 2:14-15 (NRSV)

4-30
Great Is Our God
God is too big to be confined to our houses of worship. Solomon reminds us in his prayer of dedication for the temple, "But will God indeed dwell on the earth? Behold, heaven and the highest heaven cannot contain You, how much less this house which I have built!" 1 Kings 8:27 (NASB). Paul also reminds us, "The God who made the world and all things in it,

since He is Lord of heaven and earth, does not dwell in temples made with hands" Acts 17:24 (NASB). He who is Lord of heaven and earth will not be restricted to our spaces and boxes. He moves throughout the world, even among the pagans. He dwells among His people wherever they are and goes with them wherever they go. Praise Him!

5-1
Seek Wisdom
The wisdom literature of the OT teaches us that we are to seek wisdom always. It is telling us not to learn things the hard way. As for me, I have experienced "learning the hard way" more than I want to remember. Often life will teach us by difficult experience what we could have avoided, had we been astute enough in our observations and passionate enough in our pursuit of wisdom. Our quiet times with the Spirit, our study of Scripture, and obeying the teachings of our Lord, are the wise ways to build our lives on the Rock.

The purpose of Proverbs- "To know wisdom and instruction, to discern the sayings of understanding, to receive instruction in wise behavior, Righteousness, justice and equity; to give prudence to the naive, to the youth knowledge and discretion." Pr 1:2-4 (NASB)

5-2
Present To Serve
There are parts of our journey that we may not like: unpleasant sights and sounds, cluttered and trashed places, and pathetic souls decimated by sin. What we like is to see pretty things and be uplifted by warm

feelings. God is ever trying to get us to see things through His eyes, so that we can be hearts and hands that make a difference. Unpleasant things may become opportunities to be Jesus to the hurting. Injustice may be a chance for us to show justice and mercy. We must never despise where we are, because it may make us miss what we are supposed to do and to be.

Father, forgive us for complaining about difficult places and times. Help us to be faithful in all places and at all times. May we not miss the privileges we have of serving you wherever we are today. Empower us to show your grace. Amen!

5-3
The Price Of Broken Covenant
In ancient days when two parties made a covenant, they would walk between the pieces of a divided sacrifice, saying as it were, "If this covenant is broken, this is what will happen to me." However, when God initiated the covenant with Abraham, He alone walked the pieces while His friend was in a "deep sleep" (Gen 15:12). On the cross He took on Himself the price of a shattered covenant, dying for a broken covenant and establishing a New Covenant. The cross did not take Him by surprise. He planned for it! Oh my! What love! What mercy! What grace!

"When the sun had set and darkness had fallen, a smoking firepot with a blazing torch appeared and passed between the pieces. On that day the LORD made a covenant with Abram." Genesis 15:17-18a (NIV)

5-4

Incomprehensible Peace

The beginning of our peace with God is when we realize that we have been reconciled to God through His Son Jesus (2 Cor 5:19). In justification by faith we have *peace with God* (Rom 5:1). Then the *peace of God* guards our inner persons as well as our thoughts. It presides over us in unexplainable and incomprehensible ways, even in the midst of the greatest trials of our lives. We know we have the *peace of God* and go forward to live our lives, even when all around us seems to be falling apart.

"And the *peace of God*, which surpasses all comprehension, will guard your hearts and your minds in Christ Jesus." Phil 4:7 (NASB)

5-5

Led By Silence

Sometimes we seek divine guidance that never seems to come. We ask for an answer, and get silence. Might this, within itself, be leadership? What if God is waiting to see what we will do out of love? What if He is maturing us without filling in every little detail of our lives? What if He is teaching us responsibility? What if He wants us to use our will to make free choices based on our own developing character? No, we never walk on our own. But there are many times God is waiting for us to do His teaching and to put into practice the Great Commission and the Great Commandment.

Dear Lord, forgive us for asking you to do what you have already commanded us to do. May the fullness of your Spirit in us work in seamless ways through our personality to do your work. When your work is all around us, may we, as your representatives in the world, do it with all of our hearts. Amen!

5-6
Peacemakers
Christians are called to be peacemakers. We must understand that there are many behaviors which are incompatible with peacemaking. Disrespect and unkindness gives no chance for peace. Pinning names on others is a way of discounting the opinions of the other person, resulting in further polarization. Speaking much and listening little does not help. Reactionary anger divides even more. Those at peace with God are to seek/pursue peace with all others (Ps 34:14, I Pet 3:11, Heb 12:14, Rom 12:18). God is a reconciling God and so are His true children.

"Blessed are the peacemakers: for they shall be called the children of God." Matt 5:9

5-7
A Bigger Life
Live a life that is bigger than yourself. Take on challenges that are too big for you to complete in your lifetime. You can best do this in partnership with your Father. Plant trees that will bear fruit for others to pick! Invest in enterprises that rescue the lost, feed the poor, nurture the broken and restore the downtrodden. Invest in Christ's mission. Kingdom investments will bear fruit after you have gone. People you have never known will drink water from wells you dig.

"Then Peter arose and went with them. When he was come, they brought him into the upper chamber: and all the widows stood by him weeping, and showing the coats and garments which Dorcas made, while she was with them." Acts 9:39

5-8
A Parent's Prayer
The mother of Samson, Manoah, "prayed to the LORD: 'O Lord, I beg you, let the man of God you sent to us come again to teach us how to bring up the boy who is to be born'" Judges 13:8 (NIV). The prayer of every mother and father should be, "Lord, teach me how to bring up this child." This prayer expresses dependence upon God, it implies partnership with God and is a stewardship for which we are accountable. God wants to answer this prayer. "The man of God" and the church have a role in this. Our Heavenly Father wants to be involved in parenting.

"Hear, O Israel! The LORD is our God, the LORD is one! You shall love the LORD your God with all your heart and with all your soul and with all your might. These words, which I am commanding you today, shall be on your heart. You shall teach them diligently to your sons and shall talk of them when you sit in your house and when you walk by the way and when you lie down and when you rise up." Deut 6:4-7 (NASB)

5-9
Free Will
Free will is a gift of free grace from the uncontrolling love of God. We have free choice to do right or wrong. To claim free choice, when God is always the hidden decider of even the most minute details of our lives, makes the words "free will" mean nothing. We make choices each day to help or ignore, heal or hurt, encourage or blame, fight or make peace. We are to use choice in godly ways. We are to use it based on the Golden Rule. Free will needs free grace, which makes us truly free to choose the right and the good. Right choices build character. We are responsible for how we use it and will be judged by its deeds.

"For we must all appear before the judgment seat of Christ, so that each one may be recompensed for his deeds in the body, according to what he has done, whether good or bad." 2 Corinthians 5:10 (NASB)

5-10

You Have Been Forgiven
God wants to guide you past your failures to your potential. One of the most counter-productive things we can do is to let yesterday's mistakes destroy today. Own the mistake. Confess the sin. Learn from it. Let it go. Move on. Take up your bed and walk. Receive the forgiveness of Christ. Do not hold against yourself that from which He has freed you. Hear His word of forgiveness from the cross. Keep saying to yourself, "I am forgiven."

"I am writing to you, little children, because your sins have been forgiven you for His name's sake." 1 John 2:12 (NASB)

5-11
Singing Exiles

How can we sing in a foreign land? When it is dark? When grief is overwhelming? When trials and troubles have come in like a flood? When in chains in a Philippian jail (Acts 16:25)? We can sing the Lord's song anywhere. His song recounts His faithfulness in all of our yesterdays and promises hope for all of our tomorrows. The pitch of our song comes from a heavenly place. Its melodies are prophetic poems. We sing in concert with the saints of all ages, who by faith overcame (Heb 11). Take your harp off the willow and sing!

"By the rivers of Babylon, there we sat down and wept, when we remembered Zion. Upon the willows in the midst of it we hung our harps. For there our captors demanded of us songs, and our tormentors mirth, saying, "Sing us one of the songs of Zion." How can we sing the LORD'S song in a foreign land? Psalm 137:1-4 (NASB)

5-12
Communication With The Father

Before the fall, Adam and Eve had open communication with God. Being made in the image of God, our first parents were shaped by these regular encounters. In this relationship the first humans knew who they were: those made in the divine likeness. The conversations we have with God makes us remember who we are and why we are here. Sin makes us want to hide from Him.   Time with our Father should keep us from sin's death-dealing traps. In conversations with the Father, we are regularly infused with the life of God by His Holy Spirit.

They heard the sound of the LORD God walking in the garden in the cool of the day, and the man and his wife hid themselves from the presence of the LORD God among the trees of the garden. Then the LORD God called to the man, and said to him, "Where are you?"   He said, "I heard the sound of You in the garden, and I was afraid because I was naked; so I hid myself." Genesis 3:8-10 (NASB)

5-13
Different Struggles
All of us do not spend the same amount of time in Gethsemane. The length and depth of our sorrows are not the same. If we look at others we think they have it easy. It is likely a mirage. Even if their load is lighter, it is none of our business. "What is that to you? You follow me." We do not all walk the same path but we walk with the same Lord. Our trials are different, but our destination is the same. We all have to depend on the same Lord for enough grace to get us through where we are.

Peter turned and saw the disciple whom Jesus loved following them…When Peter saw him, he said to Jesus, "Lord, what about this man?" Jesus said to him, "If it is my will that he remain until I come, what is that to you? You follow me!" John 21:20a, 21-22 (ESV)

5-14
Sin's Progression
Sin is progressive by its very nature. Once you yield to sin, it becomes easier to repeat the action the next time. Then it traps you. Sin is binding, addictive and dehumanizing. It wreaks havoc in the human personality. Sin is an intrusion into God's good creation. As we rationalize our behavior, we begin to live in false realities. A justifying reason for sinful behavior is always a lie. Avoid sin's path. It ends in distortion, decay and death.

"For the wages of sin is death, but the free gift of God is eternal life in Christ Jesus our Lord." Romans 6:23 (NASB)

5-15
What We are Becoming
We become tomorrow what we live today. We only have today to be what He wants us to be. We only have this moment to invest in His service. Time does not wait for us, and it will not excuse us. I am building the character today that I will become tomorrow. I am becoming the kind of person that I will present to my Lord on that Great Day. To waste moments and days is to waste my life.

"Be very careful, then, how you live--not as unwise but as wise, making the most of every opportunity, because the days are evil." Ephesians 5:15-16 (NIV)

5-16
Once For All

Christ died once for all. He shed his blood for all time and for all people: For those who lived before Him and for those who lived after Him. He came for sinners: All sinners. His love seeks them all. His grace includes them all. His word of forgiveness came from the cross. His gift justifies. His blood sanctifies (Hebrews 13:12). Once for all! His sacrifice needs not be repeated. It is sufficient. It is adequate today for every person, everywhere!

"Nor did he enter heaven to offer himself again and again, the way the high priest enters the Most Holy Place every year with blood that is not his own. Then Christ would have had to suffer many times since the creation of the world. But now he has appeared once for all at the end of the ages to do away with sin by the sacrifice of himself." Hebrews 9:25-26 (NIV)

5-17
Pray For All People

Pray for your enemies. Pray for political leaders. Pray for that testy neighbor. Pray for your pastor and church leaders. Christians are admonished to do all of these things. Prayers offered without love are useless. God is not interested in prayers that are arrows of anger and hate. The universe is driven by the love of God. Prayers not driven by love for all people are in vain. For yourself, pray for a new baptism of love, and then pray for all people.

"Therefore I want the men in every place to pray, lifting up holy hands, without wrath and dissension." 1 Timothy 2:8 (NASB)

5-18

Chosen For Mission

God made a choice to reach the Gentiles first through His servant, Peter (Acts 15:7). God makes choices to be carried out by servants on whom He can depend. He is always looking for willing instruments who are totally surrendered to the mission of Messiah. He found it in Paul, apostle to the Gentiles. May He find that in me! Oh, may I not discover on that Great Day what I could have done had I given Him, not just more, but all.

After there had been much debate, Peter stood up and said to them, "Brethren, you know that in the early days God made a choice among you, that by my mouth the Gentiles would hear the word of the gospel and believe." Acts 15:7 (NASB)

5-19

Reflecting The Father

We are mirrors meant to reflect the divine image and likeness of our Father. The mirror must be turned in such a way that others see the Father, and not us. This is the way we worship and witness. When our behaviors are like our Father's, we win a following for our Father and not for us. We are to be a way for others to see the glory of God through us. Angle your mirror on Him. Reflect the glory of the Father and Son by the energy of the Spirit.

"And we, who with unveiled faces all reflect the Lord's glory, are being transformed into his likeness with ever-increasing glory, which comes from the Lord, who is the Spirit." 2 Corinthians 3:18 (NIV)

5-20
All But Love

In the unsurpassed hymn, *And Can It Be*, Charles Wesley, speaking of the incarnation, said, "He emptied himself of all but love." Is that not a pattern for us? Everything in us contrary to love, everything that dilutes love, everything that keeps love off our heart's throne, must be cast down. Everything that exalts itself against God, who is love, must go. Is this not holiness of heart? This emptying of all but love is the path to which we are called.

"See how great a love the Father has bestowed on us, that we would be called children of God; and such we are" 1 John 3:1 (NASB). Beloved, if God so loved us, we ought also to love one another." 1 John 4:11 (KJV)

5-21
God And Selfies

God does not do selfies. He is concealed in the sunrise and hides behind the sunset. He is in the blooming of a flower and the singing of a bird. He is in the majesty of the storm and the calm gentle shower. The rivers, the waterfalls, the jagged cliffs and the placid lakes testify of Him. He is in a baby's smile. He comes to us in the poor and needy. Because He does not do selfies, some say that He is not there. The image of a single snapshot would so limit the great I AM. I have seen Him who is unseen. I have felt His Presence, when it could only have been Him.

"He was in the world, and the world came into being through him; yet the world did not know him." John 1:10 (NRSV)

5-22
Ask For Wisdom
In the Letter of James we are invited to ask for wisdom. In the Proverbs we are to seek wisdom. There is a wisdom that is higher than ours. It can touch our imagination and inspire us. It can be the source of new thoughts and ideas. This wisdom which is above us and beyond us is available to us. Sometimes it is hard to see and hear it when our little thoughts eclipse it. But Wisdom is there. We are to ask for it and seek it.

"But if any of you lacks wisdom, let him ask of God, who gives to all generously and without reproach, and it will be given to him." James 1:5 (NASB)

5-23
Process And Forgiving
It is not easy for a person who has suffered some great injury to forgive the other person. Most of the time forgiveness cannot happen on the day of the crime or injury. Forgiveness is the end of a painful process. Yet, even while Jesus was being crucified, He was saying, "Father forgive them. They do not know what they are doing" (Luke 23:34). This was no painless forgiving! The Father had already grieved over human sin. The process of forgiveness was eternally settled in the heart of the Father and His Son when the Son left heaven. Hallelujah, what a Savior!

5-24
Prince Of Peace Weapons
We cannot and will not advance the Kingdom of God by our angry rhetoric. We have not been alone enough with Messiah to catch His Spirit. The Kingdom of God advances through love, peacemaking, meekness, and humility, as taught in the Sermon on the Mount. This sermon is the spiritual warfare strategy for the Kingdom of God. It is the way that we live counter-culturally. We must be so saturated with the virtues of the Kingdom of God that we will not negatively reflect on our Lord, the Prince of Peace.

"For if you love those who love you, what reward do you have? Do not even the tax collectors do the same?" Matthew 5:46 (NASB)

5-25
The Coming Kingdom
Before the ascension, the disciples were ready for Jesus to restore the Kingdom to Israel immediately. Jesus reminded them that restoration was in the realm of God's timing. Yet, they were about to experience the true power and authority of the Kingdom in the outpoured Spirit. While we pray, "Thy Kingdom come," we are to live the Kingdom *now* in the power and authority of the Spirit. This is because the life of the King of the Kingdom is now enthroned in us. Jesus is saying that what the future Kingdom will look like is what we are to be living in the present.

So when they had come together, they asked him, "Lord, will you at this time restore the kingdom to Israel?" He said to them, "It is not for you to know

times or seasons that the Father has fixed by his own
authority. But you will receive power when the Holy
Spirit has come upon you, and you will be my
witnesses in Jerusalem and in all Judea and Samaria,
and to the end of the earth." Acts 1:6-8 (ESV)

5-26
Tasty Fruit
Forbidden fruit is tasty. To partake is to be shaped by
it. This is precisely why the commandments are given
to us to avoid sin. The commands are love's
warnings. Tasting sin creates a savory experience. It
wants more. It enslaves. Its reshaping makes us
think, "We are made for this." The new inclination
seeks to redefine who we are. It even tells us, "This
is who you are." It is a lie. Sin's actions create an
estrangement from the divine likeness, which is our
true home and destiny.

Jesus answered them, "Truly, truly, I say to you,
everyone who commits sin is the slave of sin. The
slave does not remain in the house forever; the son
does remain forever. So if the Son makes you free,
you will be free indeed." John 8:34-36 (NASB)

5-27
A Righteousness Kingdom
Paul said that we were to be "slaves of
righteousness". That is, we are to serve
righteousness by doing right (i.e. obedience) as God
declares right. We serve in view of the day when our
Lord will come and set all things right. Jesus said,
"Seek first His kingdom and His righteousness" (Mt.
6:33). Our King is a righteous King. Righteousness

and justice are the climate of the Kingdom of God. This covenant faithfulness is in the DNA of the King, and He wishes to pass it on to His children. He and His children are setting right what sin set wrong.

"Do you not know that when you present yourselves to someone as slaves for obedience, you are slaves of the one whom you obey, either of sin resulting in death, or of obedience resulting in righteousness? But thanks be to God that though you were slaves of sin, you became obedient from the heart to that form of teaching to which you were committed, and having been freed from sin, you became slaves of righteousness...For just as you presented your members as slaves to impurity and to lawlessness, resulting in further lawlessness, so now present your members as slaves to righteousness, resulting in sanctification." Rom 6:16-19 (NASB)

5-28
To Pray Or To Act

Then the LORD said to Moses, "Why are you crying out to Me? Tell the sons of Israel to go forward" (Ex14:15). "Why are you praying and not acting?" Praying cannot substitute for obedience. Piety cannot take the place of action. There is a time that we must move beyond prayer and Bible study and get on with the mission. Look out the window from your Bible study and see the hungry, the helpless and the hurting. Do not close the curtain. See the lonely, the desperate and the lost. Arise from your knees, get on your feet and get going.

5-29

Dead Faith

"Faith without works is dead" (James 2:14-26). Dead faith will not save us or the world. A fear of *works righteousness* can leave us doing nothing. Faith expresses itself by works. Works done for our Lord are an extension of faith. Without works, our profession of faith is vain. Without the marriage of faith and works, there is no justification (James 1:24); there are no works done in righteousness. The righteous practice acts of righteousness, which is living by faith (Rom 1:17, Gal 3:11).

5-30

Land Of Grace

We have come into a land that already had grapes and fruit in abundance. We drink from wells that we did not dig. We inherited a good land. The Lord fought for us. It is a land won for us by our Joshua, Jesus. He did it for us as a free gift of grace. We do not boast in anything we have. If it were not for Him, we would still be slaves of sin, living without Exodus. He brought us out and brought us to Himself. We live in the Promised Land of Grace!

"So I gave you a land on which you did not toil and cities you did not build; and you live in them and eat from vineyards and olive groves that you did not plant. Now fear the LORD and serve him with all faithfulness. Throw away the gods your forefathers worshiped beyond the River and in Egypt, and serve the LORD." Joshua 24:13-14 (NIV)

5-31
Seeing In The Dark
The dark times of our lives tend to frighten us, because we cannot see what lies around us nor before us. The darkness and the light are the same to our Lord (Ps 139:12). We assume because it is dark that the Light of the World is somewhere else. It is not so. On Holy Saturday the Light of the World entered darkness. Darkness cannot hide Him, nor put out His Light. We learn to see Him in the dark in ways that we can never see Him in the light.

If I say, "Surely the darkness shall cover me, and the light around me become night," even the darkness is not dark to you; the night is as bright as the day, for darkness is as light to you." Psalm 139:11-12 (NRSV)

6-1
Highways To Zion
Without an internal compass, we can get off the road. Without knowing the right road when we see it, we are clueless. There is to be a way in our heart that longs for the Lord's way. Having traveled this road, we desire it. As we grow, its map is imprinted on us. As we travel, the Way forms us. We learn by the practice of habit to stay on the Way. We also learn to avoid practices that can take us away from the High Road. The Spirit in us keeps us "Marching to Zion".

"How blessed is the man whose strength is in You, In whose heart are the highways to Zion!...They go from strength to strength, every one of them appears before God in Zion." (Psalm 84:5 & 7 NASB)

6-2

One In Our Sorrows

When Jesus became incarnate with us, He experienced the full human condition. He came into our loneliness; no one tarried to pray with Him. He felt our abandonment and cried, "My God, why have You forsaken me?" He embraced our pain when He embraced the cross. He knew rejection. "He came to His own and His own did not receive Him." He was betrayed. He was denied. His love was spurned. He knew misunderstanding. His family thought He was crazy. *He came into all of this so that we can come to Him in all of this.* We make ourselves one with Him who made Himself one with us.

"He was despised and rejected by men; a man of sorrows, and acquainted with grief; and as one from whom men hide their faces he was despised, and we esteemed him not. Surely he has borne our griefs and carried our sorrows; yet we esteemed him stricken, smitten by God, and afflicted. Isaiah 53:3-4 (ESV)

6-3

My Pierced Ear

I was a slave, and He set me free. How will I use this freedom? I will use this freedom in love to serve my Master, the One who freed me. I will not go out on my own from Him. I will ask Him to pierce my ear, so that all will know that I am His slave. How could I leave my Father's house and go out from Him? How could I not give my life for the One who saved my life? I can never fully repay Him, but I can serve Him. I can love Him and worship Him with all my heart, soul, mind and strength.

"You shall remember that you were a slave in the land of Egypt, and the LORD your God redeemed you; therefore I command you this today. It shall come about if he (*a slave*) says to you, 'I will not go out from you,' because he loves you and your household, since he fares well with you; then you shall take an awl and pierce it through his ear into the door, and he shall be your servant forever. Also you shall do likewise to your maidservant." Deut 15:15-17 (NASB)

6-4
Filled With The Spirit

"All of them were filled with the Holy Spirit and began to speak in other languages, as the Spirit gave them ability" Acts 2:4 (NRSV). Fourteen different ethnic groups heard good news in their own particular dialect without the aid of an interpreter. This was a *sign to unbelievers* that made them believers (I Cor 14:22). The filling of the Spirit was radically cross-cultural, bringing ethnic groups together in unity under the Lordship of Messiah. Pentecost's vision is to bring all people groups together as one new humanity in Jesus.

Holy Spirit, break down the ethnic and cultural barriers by your filling. Pour out your love in us (Rom 5:5) so that we may love all people groups in Your power. Amen!

6-5
Promptings Of The Spirit (1), To Ourselves

The Holy Spirit is connected to us at the deepest level of who we are. He knows us better than we know ourselves. He is with us to prompt us to follow Jesus in all the ways we are not yet following Him. Attentiveness, to follow Him always by willing obedience, is required in this relationship. His promptings correct us. He calls us out of ourselves into Himself. He calls us away from sinful gratifications to meeting the needs of family and peers.

"But I say, walk by the Spirit, and you will not carry out the desire of the flesh." Gal 5:16 (NASB)

6-6
Promptings Of The Spirit (2),
In Our Relationships
When we are in tune with the Spirit, he helps us to see people needs around us. He prompts us to respond to these needs with our words and actions. He shapes us to be the kind of persons that will respond. The Father is looking for His kingdom citizens to make a difference in the world every day and every moment. We can only do this if we are in tune with the Father's agenda. The grace of the Spirit in us, and in others, is the Catalyst we need for healing in our world.

Who led them through the depths?...The Spirit of the LORD gave them rest. So You led Your people, To make for Yourself a glorious name." Isaiah 63:13a, 14b (NASB)

6-7
Promptings Of The Spirit (3), In Prayer
Stories abound about a person in one part of the world being prompted to pray for a person in another part of the world and God rescuing in time of crisis. Somehow, in some inexplicable way, these promptings are important in God's work in the world. Power and protection is released through prayer. Working with God in these things is a "wrestling" that is not with flesh and blood. All believers are in solidarity with each other, and the Spirit prompts us for the furtherance of God's plan in the world.

Then the Spirit said to Philip, "Go up and join this chariot." Acts 8:29 (NASB)

6-8
Spirituality And Physicality
The Holy Spirit dwells in our deep inner self so that the body becomes the temple of the Holy Spirit. Our relationship with God is about physicality as well as spirituality. Jesus Messiah was God in the flesh. The God who dwelt in Jesus wants to dwell in you, without rival, and make your body His sanctuary. Since your body is His temple, He wants you to depart from the unholy. Do not engage with anything that is contrary to your being a temple in which the Holy God dwells.

"Or do you not know that your body is a temple of the Holy Spirit within you, whom you have from God? You are not your own, for you were bought with a price. So glorify God in your body." 1 Corinthians 6:19-20 (ESV)

6-9
Joy And Glory
Does your joy have glory in it? Is there something in it beyond your immediate happiness? Is this joy with you in spite of your circumstances? Does your joy have in it an element of unexplainable mystery and inexpressible words? Peter spoke of joy with glory in it. Glory, the manifest presence of God, not only hovers over us and around us, it is in us by the Holy Spirit. In the Kingdom of God we have "peace and joy in the Holy Spirit" (Rom 14:17). The presence of God's glory in us is the real secret of our joy.

"Though you have not seen Him, you love Him, and though you do not see Him now, but believe in Him, you greatly rejoice with joy inexpressible and full of glory, obtaining as the outcome of your faith the salvation of your souls." 1 Peter 1:8-9 (NASB)

6-10
Christ The New Temple
In the ancient temple of Israel there were separate courts (areas) for priests, for men, for women and for Gentiles. These barriers were all shattered when Christ, the New Temple, was raised from the dead. Jesus said, "Destroy this temple, and in three days I will raise it up" (Jn 2:19). Being baptized into Him means that the walls of class, gender and ethnicity are broken down. In Him, all have a place of acceptance, redemption and service. In Him, we are a royal priesthood and a holy nation (I Pet 2:9). In the Body of Christ (The Temple), the world's divisions are set aside and the Father's vision for unity comes! Hallelujah!

"For all of you who were baptized into Christ have clothed yourselves with Christ. There is neither Jew nor Greek, there is neither slave nor free man, there is neither male nor female; for you are all one in Christ Jesus" Gal 3:27-28 (NASB).

6-11
Drawn To The Father
Trinity Sunday: The Father sent His Son, and then, through the exalted Son poured out His Spirit on the day of Pentecost, so that He might draw the world back to the Father through the Son and the Spirit. This *drawing through the Spirit and the Son* is our salvation and redemption. The whole Trinity is involved in everything God does in our lives. This Trinitarian plan is the way that the Father, Son and Spirit are redeeming all things from the fall and setting the stage for New Creation.

"This Jesus God raised up again, to which we are all witnesses. Therefore having been exalted to the right hand of God, and having received from the Father the promise of the Holy Spirit, He has poured forth this which you both see and hear." Acts 2:32-33 (NASB)

6-12
We Are Temples
"Do you not know that you are a temple of God and that the Spirit of God dwells in you?" (I Cor 3:16). The indwelling Spirit, among other things, is about us becoming temples. We are temples in which God dwells as He dwelt in the tabernacle in the wilderness. We are temples in which prayers are offered, "without

101

ceasing" (I Thess 5:17). We are temples where heaven and earth, God and humans, meet. By being in-dwelt by the Spirit of God, we touch this world with the Life of Heaven. This is what Christians are to be for the world around us.

6-13
Ask For The Spirit
Jesus invites us to ask the Father for the Spirit. This is more than a one-time asking, as we see in the refilling of the disciples (Acts 4:31). This asking is at the heart of our prayer life. It is knowing how much we need the Lord and His inner strength. It is the cure for self-sufficiency. It is the path to power and boldness. It is God's plan of filling our heart and personality with Himself. We are invited to "ask for the Spirit". We are in desperate need of this Gift. Oh Father, fill us anew and afresh with Your Holy Self!

"If you then, who are evil, know how to give good gifts to your children, how much more will the heavenly Father give the Holy Spirit to those who ask him!" Luke 11:13 (NRSV)

6-14
The Spirit And Testimony
The presence of the Spirit of Jesus has the power to draw people to the Father. The presence of the Spirit in our lives is winsome. When He is at work in us, He is drawing people to Christ, even when we are not conscious of it. Our witness should always give room for Him to work. Some of our evangelistic methods show little confidence in the real inner workings of the Spirit. The Spirit is always at work, validating the truth

of Jesus. We tell our story, we seek to persuade, but it is the Spirit who convinces.

"When the Helper comes, whom I will send to you from the Father, that is the Spirit of truth who proceeds from the Father, He will testify about Me, and you will testify also, because you have been with Me from the beginning." John 15:26-27 (NASB)

6-15
Unity Of The Spirit
Our unity with one another is anchored in the unity that exists in the Holy Trinity. The Father, Son and Spirit live in complete unity. The Spirit in us seeks to bring this kind of unity to our faith communities. When the Spirit works in us unhindered, He will bring us together in the family of God, in spite of our political, cultural, and personal differences. We desperately need to let the Spirit heal the divisions that exist among us and bring us to real unity in the Spirit.

"Therefore I, the prisoner of the Lord, implore you to walk in a manner worthy of the calling with which you have been called, with all humility and gentleness, with patience, showing tolerance for one another in love, being diligent to preserve the unity of the Spirit in the bond of peace. There is one body and one Spirit, just as also you were called in one hope of your calling; one Lord, one faith, one baptism, one God and Father of all who is over all and through all and in all." Ephesians 4:1-6 (NASB)

6-16
Spirit Power
The Spirit of God is a burning, sending, empowering force. We cannot harness Him. We cannot use Him for our agendas. We cannot impose our will on Him. We can only let Him do what He intends to do with us. We do not want to grieve Him or quench Him in His work. May He sweep us along in the grand move of what He is trying to do with all humanity. May we be an open channel through which this mighty River can flow.

"And my message and my preaching were not in persuasive words of wisdom, but in demonstration of the Spirit and of power, so that your faith would not rest on the wisdom of men, but on the power of God." 1 Corinthians 2:4-5 (NASB)

6-17
The Healing Tree
After the Exodus, a pool of bitter water was made sweet by casting a particular tree into it. This tree was a type of healing. The church, through the years, has seen this tree as pointing to the cross. Because of that tree, we have the Water that gives life. Following the way of the cross, there is healing and health from the diseases belonging to the house of bondage. Following the way of the cross makes us dispensers of the sweet life-giving water promised by Jesus (Jn 4:14).

The LORD showed him (Moses) a tree; and he threw it into the waters, and the waters became sweet...And He said, "If you will give earnest heed to the voice of the LORD your God, and do what is right in His sight, and give ear to His commandments, and keep all His statutes, I will put none of the diseases on you which I have put on the Egyptians; for I, the LORD, am your healer." Ex 15:25-26 (NASB)

6-18
Health Food
We are learning that what we eat affects our health. We do not live by bread alone but by *every word* of the Lord (Deut 8:3, Mt 4:4, Lu 4:4). We may tend to be selective in what words we consume from the Lord. Some words may be bitter to the taste but sweet to the soul. We need every word. We need the Living Word which will give us life and health. Jesus is the Bread, come down from heaven, given for the life of the world. Avoid spiritual junk food and feed on the Living Bread for your spiritual health.

"This is the bread which comes down out of heaven, so that one may eat of it and not die. I am the living bread that came down out of heaven; if anyone eats of this bread, he will live forever; and the bread also which I will give for the life of the world is My flesh." John 6:50-51 (NASB)

6-19
Healing Waters
Naaman, the Syrian leper, found healing through a seven-fold baptism in the Jordan River (2 Kings 5:14). Jesus became the healing waters for the man at the pool of Bethesda (Jn 5:8). Our baptism into Jesus is a soul-healing plunge. He is the Stream in which we are ever washed. Jesus is the river Ezekiel saw flowing from the sanctuary (Ezek 47:12). He is the

Stream that heals our diseased souls. This Stream brings about wholeness and holiness.

"Oh, the joy of sins forgiven!
Oh, the bliss the Blood-washed know!
Oh, the peace akin to heaven,
Where the healing waters flow!

"Cleansed from every sin and stain,
Whiter than the driven snow,
Now I sing my sweet refrain,
Where the healing waters flow!

"Where the healing waters flow!
Where the joys celestial glow,
Oh, there's peace and rest and love,
Where the healing waters flow!"

- H. H. Heimar.

6-20
Rehabilitation And Healing

The act of sin is an act of rebellion against the commands of the Lord. Rebellion does something in our spirit that brings disease to the soul. By faith, the offering of Jesus on the cross forgives sin, then the Spirit of Jesus, our Great Physician, comes to reside in us to heal our souls from the damage done by sinning. This includes a rehabilitation process of training damaged spiritual muscles. We practice becoming obedient servants, no longer rebels. In this way, grace works in our lives, restoring us to be like the Obedient Son.

"Bless the LORD, O my soul, and forget not all his benefits--who forgives all your sins and heals all your diseases, who redeems your life from the pit and crowns you with love and compassion" Psalm 103:2-4.

6-21
A Heart Of Wisdom
Psalm 90 is breathtaking in its beauty.   In it the shortness of our days are contrasted to our God, who is from "everlasting to everlasting" (v. 2).   We may make it to 70 or 80, and then we are gone (v. 10). Like withered grass (v.5), even dust calls us back (v.3), but as for our God, a thousand years is just like yesterday (v. 4).   Look at it one way, and you despair.   Look at it another way, and there is hope.   Some day we will stand before our God.   "So teach us to number our days, that we may present to You a heart of wisdom" (v. 10, NASB).   On that day, as an act of worship, may we present to Him what we have become.

6-22
One New Nation
Christians are members of one new nation, no matter their geographic location on the planet.   The Lord of this new nation is Lord above all lords and thus has our ultimate allegiance.   Our confession is, "Jesus is Lord!" This new nation is *in Messiah*.   Those *in Him* may not divide themselves by class, ethnicity or gender (Gal 3:27-28).   Any wedge that seeks to divide God's Nation/Kingdom must be soundly rejected as a spike driven into the body of Christ.   We can never, anywhere or anytime, promote the divisions King Messiah has broken down.

"But you are a chosen people, a royal priesthood, a holy nation, a people belonging to God, that you may declare the praises of him who called you out of darkness into his wonderful light". 1 Peter 2:9 (NIV)

6-23
Pleasing Yourself

We live in a time where the great mantra is, "Please yourself." This does not work according to the Christian blueprint for community. We know that we are to serve each other, but we have forgotten that; "not offending" the weak among us (Rom 14:15-21) is also a form of serving. "It is good not to eat meat or to drink wine, or to do anything by which your brother stumbles" (Rom 14:21). Reckless individualism dismembers Christ's body and can destroy community.

"We who are strong have an obligation to bear with the failings of the weak, and not to please ourselves. Let each of us please his neighbor for his good, to build him up. For Christ did not please himself." Romans 15:1-3a (ESV)

6-24
Scripture And Hope

"For whatever was written in former days was written for our instruction, that through endurance and through the encouragement of the Scriptures, we might have hope". Rom 15:4 (ESV). The Scriptures are written to bring us to Messiah and to instruct us in His ways. We need this Book to know how to live. We need the Spirit of this Book to "guide us into all truth" (Jn 16:13). The promises of the Book reaffirm our hope in the Lord, who gives us hope in all of our circumstances by His resurrection from the dead.

6-25
The Unity Of One Voice

The divisions and factions of popular culture can work their way into the community of believers. Satan rejoices! A fractured church cannot speak with one voice to the world. Paul said, "Live in such harmony with one another, in accord with Christ Jesus, that together you may with one voice glorify the God and Father of our Lord Jesus Christ". Rom 15:5b-6 (ESV). The unity of the community of faith is no little thing with God. We fight over sports and politics. Leave outside the holy place the personal opinions over which we fight. Divisions hinder worship. It grieves the Spirit of Unity, robs us of power and hurts Christ's cause.

6-26
Truth Guides

Truth is greater than what we think. Truth sits above and judges, so called, *your truth* and *my truth*. What we think is truth may not be truth at all. "There is a way that seems right to a person, but its end is the way to death" Pro14:12 (NRSV). I want to know "God's truth." I desire for my thoughts to be judged by His thoughts. I want to walk in His way and not my way. His Way is above my way. I want the Truth that will bring me to my Father's house. Lord Jesus, I am destined for confusion without You!

"Send forth your light and your truth, let them guide me; let them bring me to your holy mountain, to the place where you dwell." Psalm 43:3 (NIV)

6-27
Pride In God's Work

There are some good works that may leave us with wrongful pride. Yet, there are works, when done *In Christ* and the power of His Spirit, that give us great satisfaction. It is never, "Look at what I have done," but rather, "Look at what God has done through me." I cannot take credit for that, but I can feel good about that. I cannot say, "Look at me", but I can say, "Look at what our Great God is doing." We need that kind of satisfaction. In that, we can always rejoice.

"In Christ Jesus, then, I have reason to be proud of my work for God. For I will not venture to speak of anything except what Christ has accomplished through me to bring the Gentiles to obedience—by word and deed, by the power of signs and wonders, by the power of the Spirit of God." Rom 15:17-19a (ESV).

6-28
God's Story

We are called to be part of God's story. We hear His story. We enter it. We re-tell it. We soak in His story so our story will reflect Him. We become a participant in the story of God. The book of Acts is the continuing story of God's Spirit acting in His people throughout the world. The Epistles document it. It does not end with the Bible. It continues for all who follow the world's true King. It will not end until our King comes.

Oh Lord, thank you for including us in Your story. Help us to live it well and tell it well. Teach us how to include everyone. You do not want anyone to be left out of Your story. Help us to be a catalyst to transform the stories of those in our sphere of influence. Amen!

6-29
The Fountain Of Eternal Life
The Holy Spirit becomes in us, "A well of water springing up to eternal life" (Jn 4:14). We cannot separate eternal life from the indwelling Spirit. It was the Spirit that gave life to clay when humanity was born. It is the Spirit that gives life to the body of Christ, the Church. It is the Spirit that brings life to the individual believer. This Spirit that raised Jesus to life lives in us to bring us the eternal life that is in Christ. The Spirit is the Breath of God, which we need for our every breath. He is the Life of the soul. It is the Spirit that makes our spirit live.

6-30
Holy Boldness
We are too intimidated by the culture's limitations and parameters it seeks to impose on us. The culture seeks to move us to silence. It seeks to relegate the message of Christianity to the ash heap of history. It insists that believers *be quiet* and keep their faith *private*. The nature of the message is such that it must not be silent or private. In every generation we must break out and say, "We cannot but speak the things that we have seen and heard" (Acts 4:20). We need the Spirit to embolden us to do that.

"And now, Lord, take note of their threats, and grant that Your bond-servants may speak Your word with all confidence, while You extend Your hand to heal, and signs and wonders take place through the name of Your holy servant Jesus." And when they had prayed, the place where they had gathered together was shaken, and they were all filled with the Holy Spirit and began to speak the word of God with boldness." Acts 4:29-31 (NASB)

7-1
Rescuing Captives Of Satan
Thinking that leads away from truth leads toward captivity. Actions that lead away from obedience leave us in bondage. Satan promises pleasure, and then celebrates our addictions. He promises freedom, and gives chains. As an angel of light, he promises knowledge, and then leads us to confusion, of which he is author. A key part of the work of the Kingdom of God is to bring trapped souls out of captivity by gentle instruction in truth and careful soul care.

To pastors Paul wrote, "Those who oppose him he must gently instruct, in the hope that God will grant them repentance leading them to a knowledge of the truth, and that they will come to their senses and escape from the trap of the devil, who has taken them captive to do his will." 2 Timothy 2:25-26 (NIV)

7-2
Reverence For God
"The fear of the LORD is the beginning of wisdom; all those who practice it have a good understanding. His

praise endures forever!" Ps 111:10 (ESV). "The fear of the Lord" is best understood as reverence and awe. The idea is that we hold the Lord in a unique place of honor. This is the start of wisdom, the beginning of knowing. There is no real wisdom that does not take God into account. "The fool has said in his heart, 'There is no God'" (Ps 53:1). The fool is the opposite of the wise person. Holding God in holy awe saves from folly and sets us on the road to wisdom.

7-3
Holiness And Worship

Jesus was crucified outside of the city as a sign of the world's rejection of Him. We go out to Him, not just to bear His rejection, but in order to be sacrificed there with Him. He suffered there to make us holy. Receiving that sacrifice by the sacrifice of ourselves brings us to this holy relationship. It is there that you "present your bodies as a living sacrifice, holy and acceptable to God, which is your spiritual worship" (Rom 12:1). To belong entirely to God is holiness and is the highest form of worship.

"And so Jesus also suffered outside the city gate to make the people holy through his own blood. Let us, then, go to him outside the camp, bearing the disgrace he bore." Hebrews 13:12-13 (NIV)

7-4
Ministry Opportunities

Lord, give us eyes to see needs that glances never capture. Give us ears to hear cries of distress that occur in ordinary conversations. Give us a vision that sees possibilities in impossible situations. We want to know how to live in faithfulness. May we know how to use our hands in tenderness to lift burdens. Grant us discerning spirits to do thoughtful actions that provide real ministry to those around us that we often miss by our preoccupations. Amen!

"Brethren, even if anyone is caught in any trespass, you who are spiritual, restore such a one in a spirit of gentleness; each one looking to yourself, so that you too will not be tempted. Bear one another's burdens, and thereby fulfill the law of Christ. For if anyone thinks he is something when he is nothing, he deceives himself" Galatians 6:1-3 (NASB).

7-5
On To Maturity

Doing yesterday over is not possible, as much as we would like to go back and correct some things. Yesterday needs forgiveness and today needs wisdom. Yesterday's bad must be released so we can embrace the good of today. Lord, help us learn from bad decisions to make better decisions. Help us to see the tendencies that caused us to err, and may still lie hidden with potential for further failures. Examine us as we examine ourselves. Lead us to be more and more mature in You. Amen!

"Go on to maturity." (Heb 6:1)

7-6
Prayer Matters

Some do not pray, because their experiences, shaped by a particular view of God, say that prayer does not help. In this view of God, every detail is already

114

willed, decreed and predetermined. There is another view of God that sees God and humans joined in partnership, in which God commits Himself to work with humans. The OT presents God as relenting from judgment in response to prayer or repentance. We forget that the Exodus began when God said that He had "given heed to their cry." The Father, in pity, hears the cries of His children, to bring about new outcomes. Pour out your heart. Pray to Him at all times and places. His heart is with you. Prayer matters!

The LORD said, "I have surely seen the affliction of My people who are in Egypt, and have given heed to their cry because of their taskmasters, for I am aware of their sufferings." Exodus 3:7 (NASB)

7-7
Fresh Manna Or Stale Manna
In the wilderness, Israel was to gather manna everyday, except the Sabbath. None was to be kept until the next day. The Father was providing fresh bread for them every morning, but for those who tried to hoard extra, the next day found it to be foul and inedible. Yesterday's bread is not good enough for today. We need to gather today's bread for today. We need fresh manna, not stale manna. Father, give us this day our daily manna, Jesus Himself. By Your Spirit, distribute each day this fresh Bread from Heaven to our hungry souls.

Moses said to them, "Let no man leave any of it until morning." But they did not listen to Moses, and some left part of it until morning, and it bred worms and became foul; and Moses was angry with them. Exodus 16:19-20 (NASB)

7-8
Joy And Devotion
True devotion should have joy in it. There is nothing more pathetic than those whose religion is without joy. Piety without joy can be legalism or self-worship. Such persons are captives of a toxic faith. They are slaves to forms that have, long since, lost meaning. If we love the Lord, it is a joy to do His work and to wash the feet of His disciples. If we are doing it to get a promotion, then joyless vanity follows. We are left empty. Love the Lord, and serve Him with gladness.

"But now we are released from the law, having died to that which held us captive, so that we serve in the new way of the Spirit and not in the old way of the written code." Romans 7:6 (ESV)

7-9
Spiritual Worship
Calling emotionalism the work of the Spirit is a detour from real Presence. There is a passion in worship that is right and there is a sensuality in worship that is about us and not about Him. We do not work up what has already come down. We do not generate the Power; we are acted on by the Power. We cannot manipulate the Spirit, even by our best praise and worship. We are to "worship in spirit and in truth." We need rich theological truth to keep our spirit on the right path. We need the moving of the Spirit, or our theology becomes empty. The Spirit anoints truth.

"Yet a time is coming and has now come when the true worshipers will worship the Father in spirit and truth, for they are the kind of worshipers the Father seeks.   God is spirit, and his worshipers must worship in spirit and in truth." John 4:23-24 (NIV)

7-10
Distorting Scripture
The Bible was written over hundreds of years within cultures and with a worldview much different from our own. We tend to bring our culture to the Bible to find out what it means. Certainly the Book speaks to all ages and situations, but lazy methods of interpreting and applying often send us in the wrong direction. First, we need to sit where they sat to hear what the Lord is saying to our time.   We need the work of biblical scholars, faithful pastors and careful teachers. There must be more than "private interpretation" (KJV). We need to interpret Scripture as the body of Christ, through the lens of Christ, by the Spirit of Christ.

"But know this first of all, that no prophecy of Scripture is a matter of one's private interpretation, for no prophecy was ever made by an act of human will, but humans moved by the Holy Spirit spoke from God." 2 Peter 1:20-21

7-11
A Recipe For Worship
In Exodus 30, there were precise recipes for anointing oil and incense. Persons who made either one by this sacred recipe to be used in secular places were to be "cut off from the people" (vv 33 & 38). What is going

on here? God is unique, in a category all by Himself. We love and worship Him like no other and serve Him in the awesomeness of His holiness. The veneration of our Lord is a perfume set apart from all others and has its own holy fragrance.

"Whoever makes perfume like it and whoever puts it on anyone other than a priest must be cut off from his people...Do not make any incense with this formula for yourselves; consider it holy to the LORD. Whoever makes any like it to enjoy its fragrance must be cut off from his people." Exodus 30:33, 37-38 (NIV)

7-12
Freeing Power
Paul's problem with "sin that dwells in me" (Rom 7:20) was solved when "the law of the Spirit of life in Christ Jesus" set him free. We need the power of the indwelling Spirit to free us from the power of indwelling sin. We need the mind-set of the Spirit to defeat the mind-set of the flesh (Rom 8:6). We need the sincerity the Spirit brings to defeat our tendencies toward hypocrisy. We need His love in us to free us from jealousy and resentment. The Spirit brings power to walk away from death and falseness to life and genuineness, away from soul disease to health, wholeness and holiness.

"The law of the Spirit of life in Christ Jesus has set you free from the law of sin and of death. For what the Law could not do, weak as it was through the flesh, God did: sending His own Son in the likeness of sinful flesh and as an offering for sin, He condemned sin in the flesh, so that the requirement of the Law might be fulfilled in us, who do not walk according to the flesh but according to the Spirit." Romans 8:2-4 (NASB)

7-13
Let Light Arise
"Light arises in the darkness for the upright; He is gracious and compassionate and righteous" Psalm 112:4 (NASB). Darkness can come and settle on our souls, leaving us unable to move, because we do not know which way to step. Sometimes the darkness is so powerful that it seems to be in us and not just around us. God is in the darkness with us. Keep trusting Him. He can cause light to arise. He can calm our spirits. We must not focus on the dark but on the One who is with us.

7-14
From Our Sins
How does Jesus save us from our sins? He offers us forgiveness, but there is much more. He came to break sin's power. He came to heal sin's disease. He leads us to break sin's ingrained patterns. He came to give us a principle of love within, which is the fulfillment of the law. Sin is a failure to love. "Love covers a multitude of sins." When we are acting out of love for God and one another, sin, in its loveless ways, is displaced by love. Jesus sent us His Spirit, a principle of love within, that provides the victory which the resurrection promises.

"Above all, keep fervent in your love for one another, because love covers a multitude of sins." 1 Peter 4:8 (NASB)

7-15
Not To Us
"Not to us, O LORD, not to us, but to Your name give glory" Ps 115:1. Do not be taking credit that belongs to God. Where would you be without redemption, gifts, life, breath, strength and health? He has given you a thousand hidden benefits. In humility, bow. With gratitude from the heart, give thanks. In worship, sing. It is because of Him that we are not still held in Egyptian slavery. It is because of Him that we partake of Canaan's milk and honey. He has brought us to a good place. Not to us! To You, Oh Lord, we give glory!

7-16
Following Jesus
The religion that disconnects me from a needy world around me is not the "faith once delivered to the saints" (Jude 1:3). The religion that makes me withdraw from the leper and others I deem unclean is not the religion of Jesus. The religion that allows cultural forces to keep me from embracing the alien, stranger and giving food and drink to my enemy is not the historic Christian faith. I am not free to think, say or do as I please, since I am a follower of Jesus. His teachings are as radical today as they were to the culture of His own day. Following Him may ostracize me from my peers.

Jesus repeatedly said, "Follow Me"

7-17
Going To Church
The church is not the place we huddle to name the many sins of the many sinners. It is not where we grandstand to condemn the already condemned. It is not the place we gather to rail against the ruling class. It is where we come to pray, "Forgive us our trespasses," to be taught the ways of Jesus, so that we do not fall back into those sins. It is the place we renew ourselves in His kind of love that takes us back into the world to hug the unhugable and love the unlovable. It is the place we depart from to go about each day, humbly meeting human need with the tender touch of Jesus and pointing them to the Savior.

7-18
Initiate Good
God is waiting on us to use the freedom He gave us to initiate something good. When we see needs, we are not to say, "What is God going to do?" Instead, we are to say, "What am I going to do for God in this situation?" We are already commissioned. We have eyes to see and ears to hear. We have gifts to use. We certainly never attempt these things in our own strength. We seek to be empowered by grace. God has released us to do His work. We head off to Asia unless the Spirit stops us and sends us to Macedonia (Acts 16:6-10).

Father, forgive us for neglecting what you have already commissioned us to do, while our egos wait for special guidance.

7-19
Watering Someone Else's Seed

There is no place for pride in God's field. We are laborers together with each other and God. You may not have planted the seed, but you can water it. You may plant the seed and pray for someone else to water it. It is very unlikely that you will be the sole influence on anyone coming to Christ. Other workers have come before you, and others will come after you. Humbly sow, patiently water and prayerfully pray for God to give the increase.

"I have planted, Apollos watered; but God gave the increase. So then neither is he that plants any thing, neither he that waters; but God that gives the increase." 1 Cor 3:6-7

7-20

Christian Humility

Christian humility does not seek advancement or recognition for itself, but rather its' Lord. It finds meaning in the shadow of Christ. It finds direction in following His steps. It is happy not to be known, if He can be made known. It is happy to be demoted, if He can be promoted. It has found a life in dying. It has discovered itself in losing itself. It knows the joy and peace that comes with surrender. It has found victory in what looked like defeat.

John the Baptizer said, "He must increase, but I must decrease." John 3:30

7-21
The Blessing of Giving
Giving for the religious spectator is usually spasmodic. For the faithful, their giving is systematic. For the radical, their giving is sacrificial. To give out of passion for mission, and love for the Lord, divides the committed from the casual. Giving frees us from the trap of being takers. It transforms us from a stagnant pool to a stream of blessing. It discovers joy in helping others and advancing Jesus' mission. It lays up treasures in heaven. It grows interest for eternity. It is an investment that is truly safe and will always keep growing.

Jesus said, 'It is more blessed to give than to receive'" (Acts 20:35).

7-22
Yearning For Worship
"My soul longed and even yearned for the courts of the LORD; My heart and my flesh sing for joy to the living God" (Ps 84:2, NASB). Passionless worship is the death knell of dying churches. There is no heartfelt shout of praise rising up. There is no vision of the holiness of God that casts us on our faces. There are no glimpses of His glory. There is no understanding of being in His sweet presence. There is no personal yearning after the Lord. Lord, please touch us with fire and revive us to worship.

"For a day in Your courts is better than a thousand outside. I would rather stand at the threshold of the house of my God than dwell in the tents of wickedness." Psalm 84:10 (NASB)

7-23
Giving Account
Yes, we will give an account of ourselves. We will give a full accounting of our motives and our actions, our thoughts and our intents. We will lay it all out to the One who already knows us, and we will be judged. For now, we need the surgery of the Word, the double-edged surgical tool that will ready us for that great day. We want Him to deal with our attitudes now. We want everything uncovered, judged and cleansed before that great day.

"For the word of God is living and active. Sharper than any double-edged sword, it penetrates even to dividing soul and spirit, joints and marrow; it judges the thoughts and attitudes of the heart. Nothing in all creation is hidden from God's sight. Everything is uncovered and laid bare before the eyes of him to whom we must give account." Hebrews 4:12-13 (NIV)

7-24
Ready To Forgive
"For You, Lord, are good, and ready to forgive, and abundant in lovingkindness to all who call upon You" Psalm 86:5 (NASB). Our Father wants you to call on Him so that you can receive His forgiveness. That forgiveness is a standing offer in the magnanimous words coming from the cross, "Father forgive them." His readiness to forgive is an expression of His grace. It is an expression of His desire for reconciliation with all of His creatures. Call on Him! Confess! He is predisposed and inclined to hear you!

7-25

Under Construction

There are things about ourselves that we need to be working on regularly. We would prefer that God would push a button and do it for us. It does not happen that way. We study to increase mental powers and our grasp for truth. We work on changing habits that produce character. We discipline ourselves to be true disciples. There are no shortcuts to these. Of course, we are workers together with God. By working with Him, we are being built into persons who reflect the image and likeness of our Lord.

"We then, as workers together with Him, also plead with you not to receive the grace of God in vain." 2 Corinthians 6:1 (NKJV)

7-26

God Will Not Forget

"Can a woman forget her nursing child and have no compassion on the son of her womb? Even these may forget, but I will not forget you" Isaiah 49:15 (NASB). For humankind, it is often, "Out of sight and out of mind." We all forget people who have once been in our lives. History is forgotten. Records are lost. Our capacity to remember is limited. Our minds fail us, but the great mind of our Father always remembers. He knows our name. The names of His own are written in Heaven. One glorious day, He who does not forget will call our names and we shall rise to be like Him, and to be with Him, in the embrace of eternal remembrance.

7-27

Hold Your Ground

We are involved in spiritual warfare. Battles can drain our strength and sometimes our resolve. It is so important to keep ground we have already taken at great cost. We often have to fight to hold what has been gained. Our enemy is cunning. He has not given up on our defeat. We hold our ground by holding to the Lord. We stand on it by standing on the promises of God's Holy Word. We never cease praying and praising. We always depend on the grace of the Spirit to enable us to stand.

"Finally, be strong in the Lord and in the strength of His might. Put on the full armor of God, so that you will be able to stand firm against the schemes of the devil. For our struggle is not against flesh and blood, but against the rulers, against the powers, against the world forces of this darkness, against the spiritual forces of wickedness in the heavenly places. Therefore, take up the full armor of God, so that you will be able to resist in the evil day, and having done everything, to stand firm." Ephesians 6:10-13 (NASB)

7-28

Be Merciful

We are to be merciful because God is merciful. We are to give mercy because we have received mercy. We are to be kind, even to ungrateful and evil persons, because that is exactly what God does. "Blessed are the merciful, for they will receive mercy" (Mt 5:7). There are consequences for not showing mercy. "For judgment will be merciless to one who has shown no mercy; mercy triumphs over judgment" James 2:13 (NASB). Being merciful is grateful worship of the Father for His vast mercy to us.

"But love your enemies, and do good, and lend, expecting nothing in return; and your reward will be great, and you will be sons of the Most High; for He Himself is kind to ungrateful and evil men. Be merciful, just as your Father is merciful." Luke 6:35-36 (NASB)

7-29
You Are Truly Loved
To grasp that we are loved is life-transforming. The love of God radiates from His being, but have we yet truly sensed it? Do we feel the embracing arms of our Father? Do we yet know how much He cares about us? We cannot fully know love's length, height, width or depth. His love is wider than the oceans, higher than the mountains and deeper than the deepest sea. It passes comprehension, but can be known. It can be experienced. The love of God is the tide that floats our boat every day. It is the wave we ride to the shores of eternal bliss.

Father, teach us how to focus on You, with the heartfelt understanding that we are loved.

7-30
Hidden Pain
Our failure to deal with hidden pain will most always cause us to inflict that pain on another. To suffer in silence does not mean that others are not affected. Our social connections are changed in positive or negative ways by how we deal with our hidden pain.

We who have been wounded can be agents of healing. In some grand mysterious way, God uses our pain to heal others. He uses our testimony of triumph as a balm for the soul for those who thought there would be no healing for them, but find now that there can be.

Father, heal us, so that we can be healing agents. Teach us, the wounded, how to pour wine and oil on the wounds of those around us. We pray this in the name of the One who was wounded for us. Amen!

7-31
Disheartening Words

Verbalizing negative thoughts can do untold harm. Pessimistic words have stopped inventions, delayed projects and defeated souls. Gloomy speeches have vanquished armies and caused nations to crumble in ruins. We will be judged by the effects our demoralizing statements have had on the lives of others. Ten spies cost a whole nation 40 years in the wilderness. They saw the giants as bigger than their God. They not only failed to enter the land themselves, their great grasshopper speech sent God's people cowering away. Be careful what you say!

"So they (the ten spies) gave out to the sons of Israel a bad report of the land which they had spied out, saying, "The land through which we have gone, in spying it out, is a land that devours its inhabitants; and all the people whom we saw in it are men of great size. "There also we saw the Nephilim (the sons of Anak are part of the Nephilim); and we became like grasshoppers in our own sight, and so we were in their sight." Numbers 13:32-33 (NASB)

8-1
The Grain Of The Universe
To live the Jesus way is to live with the grain of the universe. Creation was made to function in a certain way. To go against the grain of creation is more than getting splinters in our hand. It is to go against the way God meant things to be. Go against the grain of love and it will hurt you. Go against forgiveness and you will get bitter. Go against peace and you will live with disharmony. Humans are designed for God as surely as male and female are anatomically designed for each other. That's the grain. Sin goes against things as they were meant to be and pays the price.

"And God saw everything that he had made, and, behold, it was very good." Genesis 1:31a

8-2
Let It Pass
Jesus said, "Let it pass from me". Sometimes we pray this as well. It is not a sin to pray that prayer. The struggle can bring us to say, "Nevertheless, not as I will, but as You will." God does allow some things to pass from us. He may let us avoid some things. But He does not let us avoid everything. It is not easy to know the difference. It took a thrice repeated prayer, even for Jesus. It took real surrender for our Lord. If the cup passes, thank Him. If He does not let it pass, trust Him. The cup may just lead to our resurrection.

Then He said to them, "My soul is exceedingly sorrowful, even to death. Stay here and watch with Me." He went a little farther and fell on His face, and prayed, saying, "O My Father, if it is possible, let this cup pass from Me; nevertheless, not as I will, but as You will." Matthew 26:38-39 (NKJV)

8-3
Lean The Other Way
We are born with a lean toward self and away from God, though we have an intuitive longing for Him. This problem is solved by the actions God has chosen to take on our behalf. He died that our old self might be crucified with Christ (Rom 6:6, 11). He sent His Spirit to be enthroned at the center of our being. With the dethroning of self and the enthroning of the Spirit of God, we now have a new direction in which we lean. The Spirit in us is drawing us to the Father for genuine fellowship, loving obedience and sincere worship.

"For those who are according to the flesh set their minds on the things of the flesh, but those who are according to the Spirit, the things of the Spirit." Romans 8:5 (NASB)

8-4
Tent Of Meeting
The tabernacle was called the *tent of meeting*, because it was the place where the people would meet the Lord and the Lord would meet the people. It was "a good distance from the camp," which meant that an effort would be required to get there. We believe that our Lord is with us at all times, and He is;

but there are times that we need to go outside the camp, beyond our routines and be with Him to see His glory. Go out to meet Him; make the effort; see His glory; spend precious time in His Presence.

"Now Moses used to take the tent and pitch it outside the camp, a good distance from the camp, and he called it the tent of meeting. And everyone who sought the LORD would go out to the tent of meeting which was outside the camp." Exodus 33:7 (NASB)

8-5
Assurance For Your Journey
Moses wanted assurance for the journey to Canaan. "And He said, 'My presence shall go with you, and I will give you rest.' Then he said to Him, 'If Your presence does not go with us, do not lead us up from here'" Ex 33:14-15 (NASB). The journey would have its perils and its dangers. Life is uncertain. We never know what will befall us, nor do we know when it will. This is our plight. However, we are assured in Scripture, we are not alone. If His Presence goes with us, it is enough.

8-6
Commandments Followed Deliverance
Israel's deliverance from bondage preceded the commandments. "I am the LORD your God, who brought you out of the land of Egypt, out of the house of slavery. You shall have no other gods before Me" Ex 20:2-3 (NASB). Jesus, by the cross, became our Exodus, freeing us to obey. We love Him for the rescue He has accomplished. We love to keep His

commandments and put His teachings into practice. This is the mark of freed slaves.

"If you love Me, you will keep My commandments". John 14:15

8-7
Ultimate Fulfillment In God

It is impossible for another person to meet all of our needs. We have in ourselves longings that can only be realized by a relationship with our Heavenly Father. Trying to make another person fit in that spot is futile and frustrating. Work on the God-relationship and all others will find their proper place. He longs for you more than you long for Him. Walk with Him. Talk with Him. Enjoy quiet with Him. Thrive on just being together. This is the satisfying relationship for which we long.

Father, forgive me for placing a burden on other people that only You can bear. Help me, from this day forward, to deepen my relationship with You and find You completely fulfilling to these deep longings of mine. Show me the things that make for knowing You more fully. Amen!

8-8
Jesus' World

The world belongs to Jesus. He is its King. He loves it. He died for it. It was made good, by Him, and for Him. He wants His will done here as in Heaven. He expects His followers to do that. He is taking creation back through those who follow His agenda and not their own. His agenda is love. His methods are works of healing, feeding, liberation, restorative justice, compassionate mercy, peacemaking, creation care and loving all people. He is working to make Heaven and earth one. He has invited you to become a part of His mission.

"The creation waits in eager expectation for the sons of God to be revealed. For the creation was subjected to frustration, not by its own choice, but by the will of the one who subjected it, in hope that the creation itself will be liberated from its bondage to decay and brought into the glorious freedom of the children of God." Romans 8:19-21 (NIV)

8-9
Imperfect, But Loved
You may have been conceived in love or lust. You may have grown up in abject poverty, sufficiency or abundance. You may have been abused or nurtured. Your DNA make-up, with all of your pre-dispositions, may be a burden to you. You may feel like a misfit and out of place. But you must know this; you must not forget this, you are the Father's creation! More than that, you are His beloved child. None of His children are perfectly normal, a motley lot they are, but He loves perfectly all of His imperfect ones. Rejoice.

"As the Father has loved me, so I have loved you; abide in my love." John 15:9 (NRSV)

8-10
An Experience Or A Relationship
We crave religious experiences, encounters that give us high moments. We have even been known to try to generate these times by various methods. Religious experiences can become idolatrous substitutes for a daily relationship. No human relationships can survive solely on highs. Highs and lows do not matter. What matters is a living, vital union with our Father. It is being with Him and in Him, our spirit linked with His Spirit.

"I have made you known to them, and will continue to make you known in order that the love you have for me may be in them and that I myself may be in them." John 17:26 (NIV)

8-11
The Starting Place
No matter how much you struggle with where you are presently, it is your starting place to get to where you need to be. Do not magnify your misery. To focus on it is to celebrate it, and that leaves you stuck. Lift up the eyes of your heart. Catch a glimpse of your Father. Arise, start walking toward Him. He is not focused on where you have been, or even your failures. He is focused on forming you in beautiful new ways.

The LORD had said to Abram, "Leave your country, your people and your father's household and go to the land I will show you." Genesis 12:1 (NIV)

8-12

Witness With Confidence

Look for goodness in others. Look for the hidden Christ in their lives. Look past what they are to what they can become. The Father wants to salvage all of His own from the devil's trash heap. And they are all His own. "It is not my will that any should perish." His prevenient grace is at work in all, so look for it and work with it. Grace in the heart of the hearer is the ally of the one who gives their witness of the Lord. Work with the Spirit. He is already at work.

"The Lord is not slow about His promise, as some count slowness, but is patient toward you, not wishing for any to perish but for all to come to repentance." 2 Peter 3:9 (NASB)

8-13

Live Hand To Mouth

"Give us this day our daily bread". This is to be our prayer. It is not wise to live hand to mouth when it comes to caring for your family and your future. But it is the way we live in our relationship to God. We depend on Him every moment for every bite our soul consumes. As Israel needed to collect manna every day, none stored for tomorrow, so it is with us. The bounty and variety of food He has for us never runs out. Father, give us today the bread you have chosen for us today!

8-14

Practice Real Power

According to the Kingdom of God, real power rests in surprising places. Mercy! Humility! Love! Kindness!

Service! Grace! Real power is found in all of these. To think that greater power is found in control and domination is a satanic illusion. Mercy melts hearts. Grace gives hope. Kindness kindles gratitude. Love lowers barriers and wins enemies. This is the real power of the Spirit. The Spirit dwells in the exercise of grace. He is hidden within the giving of Christ-like love. This is world-changing power!

"May the grace of the Lord Jesus Christ, and the love of God, and the fellowship of the Holy Spirit be with you all." 2 Corinthians 13:14 (NIV)

8-15
Needing The Spirit

God knows the heart. He also knows that we need the Holy Spirit. The Father willingly gives the Holy Spirit. God, by the Spirit, purifies the heart. God makes no racial, status or gender distinctions in the need of His Spirit. We need His inner strength. We need His inner cleansing. We need His Heavenly Breath, the Spirit of God the Creator, to give us life. God, who knows your heart, knows what you need.

"And God, who knows the heart, testified to them giving them the Holy Spirit, just as He also did to us; and He made no distinction between us and them, cleansing their hearts by faith." Acts 15:8-9 (NASB)

8-16
Walking A New Path

"Neither do I condemn you. Go and sin no more." Jesus did not come to announce our execution. He took judgment on Himself and judged sin. He did not come to condone our sin, for He said, "Go and sin no more." He came to give us a new beginning. He came to allow sinners to start over on a new path. We can walk this path in freedom, because we are forgiven. We can walk it in newness of life, because of the power of grace.

"Neither do I condemn you," Jesus declared. "Go now and leave your life of sin." John 8:11 (NIV)

8-17
Love Or Nothing
To experience the infilling of the Spirit is to have the love of God shed abroad in our hearts (Romans 5:5). The gifts and miracles are nothing without love. So you have had miracles done through you!? So you believe your interpretation of Scripture is better? So you think your church is better? So you think your way of worship is better? Religion without love is a curse! Worship without love is hypocrisy! Faith without works of love is a farce! Nothing!

"If I speak in the tongues of men and of angels, but have not love, I am a noisy gong or a clanging cymbal. And if I have prophetic powers, and understand all mysteries and all knowledge, and if I have all faith, so as to remove mountains, but have not love, I am nothing. If I give away all I have, and if I deliver up my body to be burned, but have not love, I gain nothing." 1 Corinthians 13:1-3 (ESV)

8-18
You Are Called To Mission
In a time of video clips and sound bites, our focus is only for a few seconds. Before we can even think to

act on what we have learned, we are inundated with a hundred more clips. Our souls are jerked around in a paralyzing inability to act. We are manipulated to do nothing about everything. God does not call us to do everything. He gives us a mission and an assignment. May He move our hearts to action! Focus on His call. Act!

During the night Paul had a vision of a man of Macedonia standing and begging him, "Come over to Macedonia and help us." After Paul had seen the vision, we got ready at once to leave for Macedonia, concluding that God had called us to preach the gospel to them. Acts 16:9-10 (NIV)

8-19
Live What You Believe
We should live toward what we really believe. Belief must be transformed into action. Good thoughts should become good deeds. We need to act out what we believe. The will is required, but willpower is not enough. We need the Holy Spirit to help us live out what we say we believe. We need the power of God to translate our faith into works and our love into service.

But someone will say, "You have faith and I have works." Show me your faith apart from your works, and I by my works will show you my faith. James 2:18 (NRSV)

8-20
Citizens Of The Kingdom

As citizens of the The Kingdom of God we bow to its authority. We are governed by its King. We live by different rules than the culture around us. We are out to extend the rule of God. We not only pray, "Thy kingdom come, Thy will be done, on earth as it is in heaven", we are to work toward that end. We believe and practice that the "greatest is the servant of all". We betray the King when we fail to live in the ways Jesus taught us.

8-21
Calvary Love

Hateful speech! Name calling! Snarling words! Angry platitudes! Unkind remarks! Judgmental statements! None of these are to come from the lips of those who profess to be following the King of Peace. He died for all people. Where is the pity you have for the sinner, the great object of Christ's love? Have you ever looked at the horror of your own sins in the face of a holy God? Does nothing trigger you to pray for the despicable? Has your heart not yet been converted to love? We, who claim Calvary, must understand what love did there, and practice it!

Lord, forgive us when we fail to show love and kindness even to those we deem to be the worst of sinners. May we see our sins as worse than theirs. May we understand how much we break Your heart when we fail to give unconditional love the way You gave us unconditional love. May we be a catalyst for unity, in the midst of warring factions! Amen!

8-22

God Of The Future

Our God is the God of our future. He has an outcome in mind for us. He already knows the valleys we travel. He has walked the dark places before us. He has heard all of our protests about His way of doing things. We often object to what is happening in our lives. We may fantasize about more pleasant circumstances to the detriment of our present growth. He is working in our pain. He is healing our souls. He is shaping us. He is maturing us.

"God is keeping careful watch over us and the future. The Day is coming when you'll have it all—life healed and whole." 1 Peter 1:5 (The Message)

8-23

Living Like Christians

When Christians fail to act like Christians, the cause of Christ suffers. Our precious Lord is still wounded in the house of His friends. People have a general knowledge of Jesus, and they often know when Christians are not acting like Him. The early disciples' lives said that they had been with Jesus. These Jesus look-alikes were called Christians. Their manner of life pointed to Jesus. May we, as Christians, live like the Christ we say we follow!

"And the disciples were called Christians first in Antioch." Acts 11:26b (KJV)

8-24

The Politics Of The Kingdom

King Jesus was not elected. He was appointed by His Father. He entered the flesh of His subjects. His Kingdom is not a democracy. He does not rule by polls, nor advance His work by political maneuvering. His Spirit works to move hearts toward His cause. As the Suffering Servant King, He laid down His life for the people. His citizens know that no matter what earthly rulers do, Messiah still reigns. They do not fret over rulers who sit on earthly thrones. They rest in the Ruler who is over all rulers. They pray, "Thy Kingdom come!"

"Clap your hands, all you nations; shout to God with cries of joy.
How awesome is the LORD Most High, the great King over all the earth!
Sing praises to God, sing praises; sing praises to our King, sing praises.
For God is the King of all the earth; sing to him a psalm of praise.
God reigns over the nations; God is seated on his holy throne." Psalm 47:1-2,6-8 (NIV)

8-25

Trying Or Being

God does not have to try to love us. It is His nature. "God is love" (I John 4:9). This is what He wants to work in us, moving us from trying to being. When we have to try to love, we are not yet matured in love. He wants to create in us a new natural, where we do the right thing without trying, where love flows out of us because that is the person we have become. The Spirit is working to create this in us.

Lord, we were made in your image and likeness to be a loving being. We got turned in on ourselves and went astray. Oh Creator, restore us to love like You made us to love! Oh God of Love, restore us so that our love is spontaneous, intuitive and natural. Amen!

8-26
The Freeing Power Of Generosity
Generosity is not always about how much you give. It is to give from a generous heart what you have. Jesus observed the offering of the widow's two small copper coins and noted that she had given more than the rich. Generosity involves holding money and material things loosely. It is driven by love of another person or commitment to a cause. Generosity is always a heart issue. A generous heart releases the grip of the hand and frees it to open up.

"I tell you the truth," he said, "this poor widow has put in more than all the others. All these people gave their gifts out of their wealth; but she out of her poverty put in all she had to live on." Luke 21:3-4 (NIV)

8-27
Guardian Against Evil
In a world of malignant evil, we need a Guardian for our souls and spirits. Hate, discord and anger gives Satan an opportunity to work (Ephesians 4:26-27). Satan is energized by un-Christlike ways. He is gleeful over division. God is not the "author of confusion" (I Corinthians 14:33), but Satan is. Satan wants us in his energy field. Avoid his traps. Be

attentive to your own spirit. Sense what destroys your peace. Ask the God of Peace for protection.

"But the Lord is faithful, and he will strengthen and protect you from the evil one." 2 Thessalonians 3:3 (NIV)

8-28
Another Joseph
Joseph said to His brothers, "You meant it to me for evil, God meant it to me for good". Another Joseph was abandoned by His brothers, denied by His friend, sold by Judas, and crucified by Pilate. The political establishment wanted Him dead. The religious establishment wanted Him out of their way. They sent Him into captivity, beating and death. By this He went ahead of us to save lives. The powers of darkness meant it for evil. God meant it for good. This Joseph rose from the dead and reigns as King of kings. He dispenses the Bread of Heaven, enough for the whole world; He turns none away.

"As for you, you meant evil against me, but God meant it for good in order to bring about this present result, to preserve many people alive. So therefore, do not be afraid; I will provide for you and your little ones." So he comforted them and spoke kindly to them. Genesis 50:20-21 (NASB)

8-29
Expect Hardships
Becoming a Christian does not solve all of our problems. In a world hostile to Jesus, it may create a whole set of new ones. Too long we have marketed

Christianity as something that will solve all of your problems. It certainly solves the problem of sin and alienation from God. Sufferings, hardships, and persecution are the lot of those who follow Messiah. His is not the way of ease, but it is the best way.

They preached the good news in that city and won a large number of disciples. Then they returned to Lystra, Iconium and Antioch, strengthening the disciples and encouraging them to remain true to the faith. "We must go through many hardships to enter the kingdom of God," they said. Acts 14:21-22 (NIV)

8-30
The Encourager
There was a man in the New Testament church who was nicknamed, *The Encourager*. Barnabas! He encouraged the church at Antioch which was reaching the Greeks, not the "in thing" for the church in Jerusalem. The converted persecutor, Saul of Tarsus, was not trusted. Barnabas went looking for him and made him a partner in ministry. God used Barnabas and his encouraging words to shape Paul. The world was forever changed by one man who was an encourager.

"They sent Barnabas to Antioch. When he arrived and saw the evidence of the grace of God, he was glad and encouraged them all to remain true to the Lord with all their hearts. He was a good man, full of the Holy Spirit and faith, and a great number of people were brought to the Lord." Acts 11:22b-24 (NIV)

8-31
Uncomfortable Devotional Thoughts
We love devotional thoughts that give us comfort. There are certainly places and times for that. But sometimes our devotional thoughts should disturb us, call us out of lethargy, and bring us to a radical new beginning. Sometimes we need to be confronted about our comfort to move out in uneasy ways to the place of rugged obedience. Sometimes we need to hear Him say, "Oh you hypocrite! When will you awake to seek first the Kingdom? When will you sell out and give me everything?"

"But woe to you, scribes and Pharisees, hypocrites, because you shut off the kingdom of heaven from people; for you do not enter in yourselves, nor do you allow those who are entering to go in." Matthew 23:13 (NASB)

9-1
The Spirit Of This Age
Our hearts and minds have been invaded by the spirit of this present age. We are conformed and not transformed. We have ceased to be salt and light. We reflect the culture more than we reflect the Christ. We have reshaped Christ to be of no offense to our lifestyles. We have muffled His radical words. We have put words of comfort in His mouth for our chosen ways of living. He is not our puppet! He is our Lord! Surrender all to His Lordship.

Father, enable us by Your Spirit to see the real Messiah. May we see Him as He is and not the way we want Him to be! May He free us from ourselves so that we can be His bond-slaves! Amen!

9-2
Ministry Methods

"I would rather make mistakes in kindness and compassion than work miracles in unkindness and hardness," -Mother Teresa. There are methods of ministry that are unchristian. We can do great harm while we are attempting to do good. It all comes back to what is in our hearts. Love for power, acclaim and notoriety corrupts ministry. Harshness hurts the compassionate Christ. Let us give thought as to how we do the Lord's work.

Holy Spirit, work in me, Oh Spirit of Christ, so that all of my ministry may be compatible with His and so that all of my service would blend seamlessly with the attitude that was in Christ Jesus my Lord. Amen

9-3

Trust At All Times

When we allow fear, anxiety or worry to enter our spiritual house, they bring with them blinders that keep us from seeing goodness and blessings all around us. Let faith, hope and love cast them out, and with gratitude start seeing how blessed you really are. We all have problems and tendencies to overcome. That is life! Trust the Lord at all times, and in all circumstances, and peace will abide in your house.

"You will keep him in perfect peace, whose mind is stayed on You, because he trusts in You." Isaiah 26:3 (NKJV)

9-4
Mean-Speak

"You love all words that devour," said David to a boasting, evil person (Psalm 52:4 NASB). He referred to this person's tongue as a sharp razor, devising destruction. Words do have the power to destroy or build up. *Mean-speak* will not build up a child, a church or a country. Words, rightly spoken, can edify, encourage, give hope and spur onward to the good and the better. God spoke into existence the good creation. Speak your words with creative design.

Father, teach us how to use words that carve out hope. May we know how to speak fitting words to those who have been beaten up by bad words. Teach us to use words that bind up the brokenhearted, encourage the faint, and kindle love. Holy Spirit, even speak through us these words. In the Name of the life-giving Living Word, we pray!

9-5
Reciprocal Grace

"Judge not, and you will not be judged; condemn not, and you will not be condemned; forgive, and you will be forgiven" Luke 6:37 (ESV). Life has its paybacks. What we give comes back to us. We reap what we sow. We receive what we give. Give out good and it will eventually come back to you. Our actions toward others have consequences for ourselves. In the end we get treated by God like we have treated others. He has given us much grace and when we fail to appreciate it by giving it away, we are under His judgment.

9-6
Sleep Of Death

Those caught in the clutches of sin are caught in the *sleep of death*. The gospel cries out, "Wake up, sleeper!" The resurrection of Jesus has power to raise those who are in the *sleep of death*. It calls out, "Christ will give you light from your dark deeds. He will give you life from your death. Awake! A new order has come. Sin and death do not have the final word. Let Jesus' resurrection be your resurrection to a new order and a new life."

Do not participate in the unfruitful deeds of darkness, but instead even expose them; for it is disgraceful even to speak of the things which are done by them in secret. But all things become visible when they are exposed by the light, for everything that becomes visible is light. For this reason it says, "Awake, sleeper, and arise from the dead, and Christ will shine on you." Ephesians 5:11-14 (NASB)

9-7
Unreliable Feelings

Feelings are not reliable. They change with the wind. They will drag us places we should not go. They will prompt us to act inappropriately. Feelings will mock us for the minor and excuse us for the major. They will steer us off course and cause us to arrive at the wrong destination. We need something beyond feelings to guide us. We need words from our God. We need the guiding of the Spirit. We need the examples of saints who have gone before us. We need faithful friends to walk with us.

Father, our emotions do not always affirm us. Yet, we know that we are affirmed by your great love for us. Your promises are sure. You are for us and not against us. You are with us and we are not alone. Amen!

9-8
Sensual Appetites

"Meats for the belly, and the belly for meats: but God shall destroy both it and them. Now the body is not for fornication, but for the Lord; and the Lord for the body" 1 Cor 6:13 (KJV). The culture has sent out its message that sexual expression is strictly left up to personal inclinations and desires. The culture teaches us to say, "My Body belongs to me, and I can do with it as I please." The message of Holy Scripture is that our body is for the Lord, and the Lord is for the body (i.e., it is His temple). It is not to be used for forbidden sexual unions (I Cor 6:15-20). It matters to God what we do with our bodies. It even matters how we think about sex. (Mt. 5:28).

Lord, we want to belong entirely to you. Enable us to go against cultural trends and even illegitimate passions of the body to be the holy persons You died to make us.

9-9
A Person Of Prayer

If you want to be a person of prayer, start praying. Take time for prayer. Pray with others. Pray alone. Hear His whispers. Feel His heart. Let His mind get inside you. He is waiting. Pray the prayers of others. Pray the Psalms. Pray the Scriptures. Write prayers.

We lose heart when we do not pray. We give up when we do not pray. Prayer is to be the constant communication of our spirit with God. It is the set of our sail. It is the true north of our compass.

"Then Jesus told his disciples a parable to show them that they should always pray and not give up." Luke 18:1 (NIV)

9-10
Being Set Free
True Christianity is not binding but liberating. Legalism binds. Love sets free. Even surrender to the cross sets us free. Christ did not come to bring us a new religion, more rigid than the ones that preceded it. He came to give freedom through love and grace. He welcomed those who, before, had been unwelcome. He received a divorcee and adulteress at the well. He gave hope to prostitutes and prodigals. He received the destitute. He freed the demon possessed. He offered freedom to the religionists of His day. The freedom Jesus brings is truly freeing.

"Take My yoke upon you and learn from Me, for I am gentle and lowly in heart, and you will find rest for your souls." Matthew 11:29 (NKJV)

9-11
The Rock
Rocks have always been seen as places of refuge from the pursuit of one's enemies, and a hiding place when under attack. Rocks lend themselves to these images because they are strong and solid. Jesus

ended the Sermon on the Mount by contrasting rock to sand as a life's foundation. Jesus is called the cornerstone or keystone in the New Testament. He is also called the foundation stone. Build on the Rock! Flee to the Rock! Stand on the Rock! It is safe there.

"Hear my cry, O God, listen to my prayer; from the end of the earth I call to you when my heart is faint. Lead me to the rock that is higher than I, for you have been my refuge, a strong tower against the enemy." Psalm 61:1-3 (ESV)

9-12
Ministry Place
Macedonia was not where Paul had intended to go. He was led there by the Holy Spirit. We have our plans, and sometimes God intervenes to bring us His plan. God would send others east, but Paul was to go the other way for now. All believers are sent to serve. Your help is needed. Let the Holy Spirit lead you as to time and place. Wherever you are, work there. Your sent place is where you are, until God shows you otherwise.

"And a vision appeared to Paul in the night; there stood a man of Macedonia, and prayed him, saying, come over into Macedonia, and help us" (Acts 16:9, KJV).

9-13
Heart-Set
"If riches increase, do not set your heart upon them" (Psalm 62:10). We should be grateful if we have the barest of necessities of life. For some, life

affords much more than this. If this is the case, we are accountable for it in our stewardship. It can be a pitfall if our heart gets tangled up with how much we have. Believers should remember that God owns everything we possess. If our heart is set on our Lord, then what is in our hands is in His hands to dispense as He will.

9-14
God Brought You Through
Look back on your life and see what God has brought you through. It will be more times than you will ever be able to recall. Just to see how He has had His hand on our lives is encouragement for today and tomorrow. David could face a giant because God had already helped him to face a lion and a bear. The God who was with us yesterday is with us today. There is nothing too big for Him.

"Have I not commanded you? Be strong and courageous! Do not tremble or be dismayed, for the LORD your God is with you wherever you go." Joshua 1:9 (NASB)

9-15
The Life Of Eternity
We usually think of eternal life as being unending life. It is better understood as the life of eternity. The biblical word is speaking of a quality of life and not the quantity of life. It is the life of Heaven given to earthlings. We partake of the life of eternity, the life of Heaven, even now. To enter into solidarity with Christ is to enter the life of God, even as it enters us. In the incarnate Christ, the life of eternity came among us to

invite our entry into it. An open heart receives it, and the darkness is banished.

"They are darkened in their understanding, alienated from the life of God because of their ignorance and hardness of heart." Ephesians 4:18 (NRSV)

9-16
Grace And Love
Grace is love in quest of you. This is not an unhealthy co-dependent love. It is not soft, but strong. Grace is love not letting us go. Grace is love seeking our full deliverance (salvation). Grace is love washing, cleansing, and purifying the people of God. Grace is love transforming. Grace accepts us as we are but never leaves us where we are. Grace is the Spirit's energy bringing about Love's dreams for us.

"Christ also loved the church and gave Himself up for her, so that He might sanctify her, having cleansed her by the washing of water with the Word, that He might present to Himself the church in all her glory, having no spot or wrinkle or any such thing; but that she would be holy and blameless." Ephesians 5:25b-27 (NASB)

9-17
Devotions And Guilt
We sometimes struggle with our "devotional life". We carry guilt, feeling it is not often enough, nor intense enough. Devotions are not an end within themselves; they are a means to an end. Heart devotion will find devotional times. It is like wanting to be with the Lover of our Soul. We are drawn to what we love.

We have time for what we love. The Father is devoted to us and longs to be with us. We love the Father and want to be with Him. Devotional times express this relationship as well as building it.

"Preserve my life, for I am devoted to you; save your servant who trusts in you. You are my God." Psalm 86:2 (NRSV)

9-18
Negative And Positive Holiness

The simple definition of the word holy that we have all been taught is *set-apart*. We are set-apart negatively *from* something and positively *to* something. This was never meant to be a matter-of-fact legalism. It is to be a dynamic relationship of love. Because we are in this love relationship with God, we reject (set-apart from) all loves (idols) that would compete with our love for Him. We cultivate this love relationship (set-apart to) we have with the Father by being with Him and enjoying His presence. This is true holiness.

"According as he hath chosen us in him before the foundation of the world, that we should be holy and without blame before him in love" Ephesians 1:4 (KJV).

9-19
Word Shaped

We are shaped by the word. God spoke and it was. Creation was shaped by the voice of a speaking God. We were spoken into divine likeness by that same word. The speaking Living Word, our Messiah, has come to shape us by His word into His likeness. We

154

are sanctified by this word which is truth. Oh Lord, keep shaping us by your written word, the Bible, and by your Living Word, Jesus our Lord! Amen!

"Sanctify them by the truth; your word is truth." John 17:17 (NIV)

9-20
Change Can Happen
We mark people off our list that God is still shaping. The arrogant, obnoxious and overbearing ones we let go. I have seen the Lord change the arrogant, always-right person, into a humble vessel of honor. I have seen the timid and shy made into flaming evangels. The die is not set so long as the Spirit is working. Remember the change He wrought in you.

"You once were disobedient to God, but now have been shown mercy." Romans 11:30a (NASB)

9-21
Nourish Your Life
God is committed to life and making dead things live. He delights in life. He teaches us to avoid what causes death. Life must be nourished. It needs food, water and light. It needs the Bread of Heaven, the Water of Life and the Light of the World. It needs the Breath of Heaven, without which we are dust. Our life is nourished by being with our Father, by abiding in the Vine and having the life of the Vine abiding in us.

"They asked, and he brought them quail and satisfied them with the bread of heaven. He opened the rock, and water gushed out; like a river it flowed in the desert." Psalm 105:40-41 (NIV)

9-22
The Beautiful
The God of love sees a beauty in us that we cannot see in ourselves.   The Great Artist is painting an unfolding picture as we yield to Him the canvas.   He arranges contrasting colors in the painting that did not come from our imagination.   The circumstances of life fling paint on the canvass that causes us to think it is ruined.   But the Great Artist is not stopped in His work.   Out of disarray He paints design. Out of the ugly He brings beauty.

"Your vibrant beauty has gotten inside us— you've been so good to us! We're walking on air! All we are and have we owe to GOD, Holy God of Israel, our King!" Psalm 89:17-18 (The Message)

9-23
True Riches
The world promises us riches in what we can hold in our hands or put in our pockets.   True riches are found in being with our Father. It is there that we find the communion that makes us wealthy.   It is the enriching relationship. Failing to have alone time with our Father is to invest in our own spiritual poverty.

"Oh, the depth of the riches both of the wisdom and knowledge of God! How unsearchable are His judgments and unfathomable His ways!" Romans 11:33 (NASB)

9-24
God's Investment
The Spirit is God's deposit in us. He is the down payment promising more to come. The Spirit is God's grand investment in us. It is risky. We can quench the Spirit or stir up the gift. We can grieve Him or work with Him. We can resist the Spirit or yield to Him. Make room for the Spirit's work. Do not just give Him the rooms of your heart. Give Him your body, His temple, to do His work through you every day of your life. Stay vested in His Investment, and you will do well.

"Now it is God who has made us for this very purpose and has given us the Spirit as a deposit, guaranteeing what is to come." 2 Corinthians 5:5 (NIV)

9-25
The Flaw In Self Evaluation
Sometimes we may feel that our mistakes are greater than our accomplishments. We may feel that our failures are greater than our successes. We are never a good judge of what God is doing through our lives. Our perspective is limited. We are to humbly learn from our mistakes and confess our failures. We are to keep on serving, giving and loving. When we do this, someday we will be amazed at what God has wrought through us.

Father, I want too much to be a success when you want me to be faithful. Forgive me! May I learn to love you with all my heart, serve you with all my energies and leave the results to You. Amen!

9-26
Solidarity And Election
Christ is the Elect Son and we are chosen *in Him*. *In Him* we are blessed in the heavenly realms. *In Him* we have redemption and the forgiveness of sins. *In the Son* we are adopted as sons and daughters of God. *In Him* we are elect. *In Him* we have all spiritual blessings. *In Him* we are chosen for holiness. Living *in solidarity* with the Son makes "our calling and election sure" (2 Peter 1:10).

"He chose us in him before the creation of the world to be holy and blameless in his sight. In love he predestined us to be adopted as his sons through Jesus Christ, in accordance with his pleasure and will--to the praise of his glorious grace, which he has freely given us in the One he loves." Ephesians 1:4-6 (NIV)

9-27
Fear Steals Blessings
Fear is the thief of blessing. It pulls us back from risks. It closes the door to opportunity. It keeps love from blossoming. It misses blessings and stifles potential. It promises that there will be too many problems. It focuses on possible pain or failure. It buries talents. So we become paralyzed where we are, no new territory is taken because nothing is ventured. There are 365 *fear nots* in the Bible, one for everyday of your year.

"And I was afraid, and went and hid your talent in the ground. Look, there you have what is yours.' But his lord answered and said to him, 'You wicked and lazy servant, you knew that I reap where I have not sown, and gather where I have not scattered seed. So you ought to have deposited my money with the bankers, and at my coming I would have received back my own with interest." Matthew 25:25-27 (NKJV)

9-28
Thirst For God

"O God, you are my God; earnestly I seek you; my soul thirsts for you; my flesh faints for you, as in a dry and weary land where there is no water" Psalm 63:1 (ESV). We have a natural thirst for God that other things cannot satisfy. To turn toward our thirst for God and to give attention to it is the essence of fulfillment, the key to holiness and the joy of living. In this we find stability and health for our souls. He satisfies our thirst.

"If anyone is thirsty, let him come to Me and drink. He who believes in Me, as the Scripture said, 'From his innermost being will flow rivers of living water.'" But this He spoke of the Spirit, whom those who believed in Him were to receive; for the Spirit was not yet given, because Jesus was not yet glorified". John 7:37b-39.

9-29
Mutual Grip

"My soul clings to you; your right hand upholds me" Psalm 63:8 (ESV). The hand of God that grips us is the hand of grace. It is extended to us in pity and mercy. It reaches down in love. It is a strong and powerful hand. The hand with which we cling to God is the hand of faith and hope. Sometimes we hold to Him out of sheer desperation, out of necessity, for we have no other such Refuge. When we embrace Him in love, we experience the loving embrace of our Father.

9-30
The Father's Help
The love that the Father has for us is expressed in the help He gives us. It drives His rescue. It makes good come out of bad, healing out of pain and joy out of sorrow. He bends toward our fainting with divine energy. He encourages us to get up when we fall. His help is hidden in the help of others. His grace is hidden in the strength He gives us. His guidance is revealed in unexpected open doors. His provisions are revealed in the fruits of earth. He gives both help and intimacy in the gift of His Spirit.

"Behold, God is my helper; The Lord is the sustainer of my soul." Psalm 54:4 (NASB)

10-1
No Other Gods
Sometimes the Father has us relinquish a thing in our hand so that He can give us something better. Then there are times that He insists that we release a thing that should not have been in our hand in the first place. It is far too easy for things to come into our lives that compete with the preeminence of the Father. You do not have to bow to a thing for it to become an idol. An idol is anything that nudges God to one side. It may even be something that we think is good or innocent.

"You shall have no other gods before Me," means that you are to have no gods "beside Me", or "in addition to Me". The literal Hebrew is, "You shall have no other gods *in my face.*" Deuteronomy 5:7

10-2
His Banner Of Love
All the tribes of Israel had their flags, banners and standards (Nu 2 & 10). The exiles are pictured returning to the land, joyfully marching under a flag (Isa 49 & 62). The lover of the Song of Songs said, "His banner over me is love" (2:4). *The Lion of the Tribe of Judah*, the Lord of the whole earth, is reclaiming all ethnic groups under the banner of Love! The cross was the standard that lifted Jesus up. He is the *Lifted-Banner* that draws all people to Himself (John 12:32). This is the welcoming banner we march under, the standard we raise, the flag to which all are invited to commit allegiance.

The Master, GOD, says: "Look! I signal to the nations, I raise my flag to summon the people. Here they'll come: women carrying your little boys in their arms, men carrying your little girls on their shoulders....Walk out of the gates. Get going! Get the road ready for the people. Build the highway. Get at it! Clear the debris, hoist high a flag, a signal to all peoples!" Isaiah 49:22 & 62:10 (Message)

10-3
Embracing Our Imperfections
Since we are all imperfect, we need to acknowledge it. It should keep us humble, keep us confessing and keep us striving to be better. The imperfect one has

no right to be condemning other imperfect ones! How could we dare? We all have shortcomings. None of us have it all together. Accept your limitations and imperfections. Believe that God can work through your imperfect *jar of clay* to offer a drink to the thirsty.

Lord, teach me how to embrace my own imperfections in a way that I might walk humbly before You. I know that, throughout history, You have worked Your perfect plan through imperfect people. I yield all I am to You for You to use in Your way and in Your time!

10-4
Be A Giving Person
Give with a generous heart and free hand. Give as lavishly as the Father has given to you. From His hand He has given you so much. Discover the joy of giving. Let your generosity be thanksgiving to God. Become a giving person. Let your gratitude overflow by giving yourself, your time, your money and your energy. A generous heart will find ways to give. "Give and it will be given to you" Luke 6:38. We do not give to get, but we give because we love. God blesses that!

10-5
Jesus Is Lord And The Spirit
"No one can say that Jesus is Lord except by the Holy Spirit" 1 Corinthians 12:3b (NKJV). The Holy Spirit always bears witness to Jesus. He affirms Messiah to our hearts. He attests Jesus' Lordship. He convicts us of things in our lives that compete with our Lord. He enables us to yield all to Christ, truly making Him

Lord of all the hidden chambers of our hearts. We must have the Spirit to surrender our total being to Jesus. We need the Spirit's witness joined to our witness to convincingly proclaim, "Jesus is Lord."

10-6
Good Deeds
We are not saved *by* good works, but we are saved *for* good works. Our Lord Jesus went about doing good in the power of the Spirit (Acts 10:38). The widow Tabitha "was always doing good and helping the poor" (Acts 9:36). We are "not to neglect doing good" (Hebrews 13:16). Doing good is part of our witness (I Peter 2:15). Let not good works be wounded in the house of faith, dismissed as mere *works righteousness*. Faith and works are partners and not competitors.

"Do all the good you can, by all the means you can,
"In all the ways you can, in all the places you can,
"At all the times you can, to all the people you can,
"As long as you ever can." - John Wesley

10-7
The Great Turn
Jesus said to Paul, "I am sending you, to open their eyes so that they may turn from darkness to light and from the dominion of Satan to God, that they may receive forgiveness of sins and an inheritance among those who have been sanctified by faith in Me" Acts 26:17b-18 (NASB). The great turn is from blindness to seeing, from darkness to light. It is from Satan's dominion to God's kingdom. It is from guilt to

forgiveness. It is to an inheritance in the sanctified community, all through faith in Jesus.

10-8
Deep Brokenness
The brokenness of all humans includes the scars of our life experiences and the imperfect DNA that we have inherited from our fallen parents, along with all of our fallen forefathers and foremothers. Who can know the depths of our broken places except the Father Himself? We feel our fallenness. Something is *just not right* with each of us. The incarnate *Man of Sorrows* is drawn to our brokenness. Keep touching the hem of the Healer's robe!

"And when the men of that place had knowledge of him, they sent out into all that country round about, and brought unto him all that were diseased;   And besought him that they might only touch the hem of his garment: and as many as touched were made perfectly whole." Matthew 14:35-36 (KJV)

10-9
Before You Ask
Before you ask, He already knows your need. He is already predisposed to receive you.   His wisdom knows best. His grace is abundant and His love is boundless. Before you ask, know that He has been waiting for you and know that Your Intercessor is standing in for you.   Know that your words do not have to be many. He hears your words and He hears your heart. Come in faith and humility to your Father and know He will welcome you.

"When you are praying, do not heap up empty phrases as the Gentiles do; for they think that they will be heard because of their many words. Do not be like them, for your Father knows what you need before you ask him." Matthew 6:7-8 (NRSV)

10-10
Give Your Witness

"Come and hear, all who fear God, and I will tell of what He has done for my soul" Psalm 66:16 (NASB). Our propositional presentations of the gospel cannot compare with a clear witness of what God has done in our lives. The former is canned, and the latter is a true witness. If we know what God has done for us, and we have experienced His grace, then we have a story to tell. It does not have to be dynamic nor dramatic. A simple story that verbalizes our gratitude to our Lord is a powerful thing.

10-11
Ever Preparing

Our life in this world is a place of preparation. God is preparing us to serve both now and in the day when His Kingdom fully comes. He is now preparing the inner self to be clothed with a new, resurrected body. He makes us new creations for the New Creation: "new heavens and a new earth in which righteousness dwells" (2 Peter 3:13). He is "washing, cleansing and making holy" His bride (Ephesians 5:26). He is preparing us for Himself and our future in His service.

10-12
Cherished Sin And Prayer
"If I regard wickedness in my heart, The Lord will not hear" Psalm 66:18. The heart cannot hold to sin and the Lord at the same time and expect prayers to get anywhere. That heart is divided. This certainly does not mean that we have to be perfect to have our prayers heard, but it does mean that if we are holding to known sins in our lives, the prayer we need to be praying is one of confession. Willful sin destroys the relationship that prayer seeks to build.

"If I had cherished sin in my heart, the Lord would not have listened; but God has surely listened and heard my voice in prayer." Psalm 66:18-19 (NIV)

10-13
Honored
Maybe instead of looking at our assignments as *duties and obligations*, we should look at them as *privileges and blessings*. It is a privilege to represent Christ, to serve Him, and live for Him. Just think, we are His ambassadors. It is an honor to give our all to the One who gave His all for us. He held back nothing in His self-sacrificial love for us. It is an honor to let our hands become His hands that lift someone's burden.

"Serve the Lord with gladness." Psalm 100:2a

10-14
Running Away
They live their lives running away from brokenness. They run to promising cups that turn out to be

tasteless and empty. They run *to* what they do not know, away *from* what they could have known. They build their lives and dreams into a fantasy land away from pain, only to find a greater pain than what they forsook. If they could only stop running, brokenness would come to them as their Heavenly Shepherd, and they could experience rescue and mission.

Father, we know we are broken. Teach us how to live our lives in brokenness the way our Lord did. Teach us that embracing our brokenness is Your way to health and wholeness. May this way of humility, dependence and weakness be a path to true servanthood.

10-15
True Kingdom Citizens
The disciples made the kingdom about *them* when they asked to sit on Jesus' right hand and on the left. Jesus is center, but they still wanted to be the ones that flanked Him, and be *seen* as the ones closest to Him. Our attitude must be, "I am not worthy. Make me your slave. Let me be unknown if He can be known. Let me sit in the lowest place. Let me be humiliated if He can be exalted." This is what true kingdom citizens look like.

"They said unto him, Grant unto us that we may sit, one on thy right hand, and the other on thy left hand, in thy glory. But Jesus said unto them, Ye know not what ye ask: can ye drink of the cup that I drink of? and be baptized with the baptism that I am baptized with?" Mark 10:37-38 (KJV)

10-16
Give Them Something To Eat

We *turn away from* what our Shepherd *turns toward.*
We turn to better pictures, avoiding the ones that
cause us pain and call us to sacrificial action. We see
the multitudes as costly mouths to feed, and He sees
them as sheep without a shepherd. Because our
resources are so limited, we want to send them away.
The Great Shepherd takes what we have, blesses it,
and there is more than enough. He must be teaching
us a life lesson!

When it was evening, the disciples came to Him and
said, "This place is desolate and the hour is already
late; so send the crowds away, that they may go into
the villages and buy food for themselves." But Jesus
said to them, "They do not need to go away; you give
them something to eat!" Matthew 14:15-16 (NASB)

10-17
Shortcuts

There are no shortcuts when traveling with Jesus, the
Way. His is the narrow road. The broad way may
seem so much more appealing. Our old enemy will
seek to deceive us by suggesting that the pleasant
fork to the right is the one we should take; after all, he
says, "Jesus never meant for life to be so restrictive."
The easy way may turn out to be a disaster. We still
need to hear Jesus warning about right roads and
wrong roads.

"Enter through the narrow gate; for the gate is wide
and the way is broad that leads to destruction, and
there are many who enter through it. For the gate is

small and the way is narrow that leads to life, and there are few who find it" Matt 7:13-14.

10-18
Dining With Messiah
"Behold, I stand at the door and knock. If anyone hears My voice and opens the door, I will come in to him and dine with him, and he with Me" Revelation 3:20 (NKJV). The Lord wants to dine with His people. He knocks at the door awaiting admission. We are preoccupied with other things. If we will but open the door, we could give to Him our hearts full of hospitality. We could sit with Him. We could listen to Him. We could know intimate fellowship with Our Messiah King.

10-19
Soft Or Harsh Words
"A soft answer turns away wrath, But a harsh word stirs up anger" Proverbs 15:1 (NKJV). The typical response when someone is coming at you *emotionally charged* is to give back to them an *emotionally charged* response. Escalation follows. Feelings are hurt. Walls go up. Defensive positions taken. Maturity and wisdom respond quietly and calmly seeking to keep emotions in check. Soft answers take down walls, open doors for solutions, create community and make dialog possible.

10-20
Hearing God Speak
God seldom speaks in an audible voice. We hear Him in our deep inner self. Most of our hearing is

selective, colored by our own predispositions. We want to hear God affirm us and our ideas. Because of this, it is easy to distort His words. We are warned about adding to and taking from His words. If we would be often with Him and listen to His heart as revealed in His Son, we would be less apt to distort what He is saying. The God who speaks invites us to listen.

"For he is our God, and we are the people of his pasture, and the sheep of his hand. O that today you would listen to his voice!" Psalm 95:7 (NRSV)

10-21
Problem Focused
If we focus too much on our problems we get paralyzed into inactivity. Trust in the Lord. Get on with what needs to be done in your life. Serve others in the name of Jesus. If we stress over our problems, we will find it difficult to get anything done. Besides, focusing on our problems gets us stuck. Our frame of mind has become prison bars. Let it go. We face our problems in the strength of Christ, through whom we can do all things.

"I can do all things through Him who strengthens me." Philippians 4:13 (NASB)

10-22
The False Self
Thomas Merton suggests that we have a false self that needs to die and a real self that needs to blossom in the likeness of the Son. The false self betrays God and me. It has a continuous inclination

to evil. The false self must die, not so that I can say I have arrived at a higher level of religious experience. That within itself tells me that the false self has not died. We die to our false self for the life of the world as Jesus died for the life of the world (Jn 3:16). We lay our lives down as a sacrifice in worship (Rom 12:1-2), poured out for God and others. This brings the life of Christ to the world around us.

"There is a sinful self that needs to die, there is a natural self that needs to be disciplined, there is an actual self that needs to be realized." J. O. McClurkan

10-23
The Unleashed God
God can do what God chooses to do. Yet, He wants to work in and through us as humans. We are afraid to surrender to His plans. We want God on a leash so we can control Him. We are afraid of where He might take us. We like to play it safe. The unleashed God is the unquenched Spirit. God the Holy Spirit is in us, to work His will and way through us. The way is to yield my way to His way. Letting God be God does not destroy us; it sets us free.

Father, thank you for the slavery that brings freedom and for the servant-hood that brings liberty. We let go of our desire to make You our servant, so that we can be free to be your servant. Thank you for the freedom we find in being your bond-slave. Amen

10-24

Healthy Self-Image

It is possible to look in all the wrong places for self-image. Possessions! Position! Power! People! It is not who you are but Whose you are. It is not what you own but Who owns you. It is not what you can do but what He can do through you. It is not where you have been but the One who is taking you where you are going. You belong to the King. You are His beloved child. He has redeemed you at great cost! He is saving you for Himself!

"Behold what manner of love the Father bestowed upon us, that we should be called the children of God" (I Jn 3:1).

10-25

The Global Kingdom

Jesus, at His hometown Nazareth, met attitudes at their worship center that were detrimental to true worship (Lu 4:16-30). Their provincial *pride of place* was saying, "Do your miracle stuff here. We are as good as those folks down at Capernaum." Jesus confronted this, and Jewish nationalism, by reminding them that Elijah and Elisha did more miracles among the Gentiles than in Israel. Reaction? Hot anger! Get out! Kill him! Jesus left them! Unchanged! More entrenched! More patriotic! Results? They missed the real Messiah, His global kingdom and their place in it!

"Elijah was sent to none of them but only to Zarephath, in the land of Sidon, to a woman who was a widow. And there were many lepers in Israel in the time of the prophet Elisha, and none of them was cleansed, but only Naaman the Syrian." Luke 4:26-27 (ESV)

10-26
Prophetic Words
Jesus' words at Nazareth were unwelcome, so that made Him unwelcome (Lu 4:16-30). Prophetic messages in Biblical times were largely about *now* and little about the *future*. Prophetic words were not always about *soothing comfort*. It was Spirit anointed preaching that confronted pride, prejudice and presumptive sins. There was no repentance at Nazareth, so kingdom manifestations went somewhere else. Lord, make us open to your Word, even if it discomforts and disturbs us.

"When they heard these things, all in the synagogue were filled with wrath. And they rose up and drove him out of the town and brought him to the brow of the hill on which their town was built, so that they could throw him down the cliff. But passing through their midst, he went away." Luke 4:28-30 (ESV)

10-27
God Is At Work
Let's stop wringing our hands over militant Islam, communist China, and all other *looming threats*. Our inflammatory rhetoric does not help, neither does our anxiety. The world's present problems are primarily theological. Governments do not have a clue of how to solve theological problems. Messiah has the answer. Have we no confidence in the faithfulness of the Holy Spirit and the power of the Gospel? Jesus will build His church (Matt 16:18)! God is at work in

our world! Believe in Messiah and cease the hand-wringing doubt! Trust God in all things!

"They set your sanctuary on fire; they profaned the dwelling place of your name, bringing it down to the ground. They said to themselves, 'We will utterly subdue them"; they burned all the meeting places of God in the land'...Yet God my King is from of old, working salvation in the midst of the earth." Psalm 74:7-8 &12 (ESV)

10-28
Inadequacy And Sufficiency
You may be at the end of your rope; God is not.
When you are out of ideas, His creativity has just begun.
When your energy is gone, His strength is beginning.
Recognize that you are empty, and then He can fill you.
When you feel your faith is not strong enough, He is faithful.
Trust Him! Lean on Him! Draw strength from Him!

"And God is able to make all grace abound toward you; that ye, always having all sufficiency in all things, may abound to every good work." 2 Corinthians 9:8 (KJV)

10-29
The Opportunist
Satan is an opportunist. He does not fight fair. He stomps you when you are down and kicks you in the face when you are trying to get up. He will take any problem we have, put a saddle on it and ride it. He

will taunt us over our emotional scars, mock us in our mental anguish and scold us for lack of faith in our physical pain. He will use others to deliver his words. Do not fear him. Do not let his words take root. Resist him! Send him away!

"You are from God, little children, and have overcome them; because greater is He who is in you than he who is in the world." 1 John 4:4 (NASB)

10-30
Horror At Calvary
All the sin in the whole world was funneled into the body and onto the sinless soul of Jesus, as He underwent His hard baptism on the cross. It was like dung spread on a white cloth, like septic flowing into pure clear water, like violence being perpetrated on a gentle soul, like bitter hate being poured out on perfect love! Our words and analogies fail to describe what Christ underwent at the Place of the Skull. He let evil play itself out on His body and soul, and by it, He defeated evil and saved the world from the horrors of death.

"For he hath made him to be sin for us, who knew no sin; that we might be made the righteousness of God in Him." 2 Corinthians 5:21 (KJV)

10-31
Hallowed Eve
October 31 has a long history of witchcraft, the demonic, and a focus on death. This was not an appropriate celebration for Christians, since Christ had triumphed over "death, hell and the grave". Their

boast was, "Oh death, where is your victory? Oh grave, where is your sting" (I Cor 15:55). So, November 1 was set as All Saints' Day to celebrate, not the dead, but those who died in Christ and our connection to them. So, the night before All Saint's Day was called Hallowed Eve (Halloween) by the church. It was to be a holy evening to prepare to celebrate all saints. Christians can look at death's terror party and call it a *holy evening,* because Christ has taken the terror out of death.

11-1
Celebrating The Saints
In the NT all Christians are saints ("holy ones"). We are called saints, and we are called to be saints. This day celebrates saints living on earth and those who live in the presence of the Lord in heaven now. The two groups are one body. It also reminds us that Christians on earth are to live a life in the train and heritage of all the *holy ones* who have gone before us. Father, thank you for all of Your saints that have influenced and shaped our lives. We have been blessed by them.

"To all who are beloved of God in Rome, called as saints: Grace to you and peace from God our Father and the Lord Jesus Christ." Romans 1:7 (NASB)

11-2
The Coupling Of Salvation And Sanctification
"God chose you as the firstfruits to be saved, through sanctification by the Spirit" (2 Thessalonians 2:13 (ESV). Sanctification is not something that is in addition to our salvation. It is part and parcel of our

salvation. Sanctification is the action and process by which we are being made holy. We are initially made holy by faith in the Messiah. It does not stop there. It cannot stop there. There is too much in us that is unholy that must be cast out, too much that needs to be nailed to the cross, and too many patterns of un-love that must be broken. The Spirit not only guides us to sanctification, His work accomplishes it.

11-3
Comprehensive Sanctification
I grew up thinking that *entire* sanctification was *final* sanctification. *Wrong!* Entire is used only once in the NT in regard to sanctification. There, it has nothing to do with final sanctification but with comprehensive sanctification, involving the whole person, body, soul and spirit. There is no room for a dualistic sanctification where only the heart and spirit is cleansed. Biblical sanctification gathers the whole person into a relationship of belonging entirely to God. The God who calls is the one who works in us to *bring it to pass*.

"Now may the God of peace Himself sanctify you entirely; and may your spirit and soul and body be preserved complete, without blame at the coming of our Lord Jesus Christ. Faithful is He who calls you, and He also will bring it to pass." 1 Thessalonians 5:23-24 (NASB)

11-4
Willful Sin
God in His faithfulness sends His commands to avoid willful sin. A positive side of these commandments is

intent on bringing about character development. They invite us to places where life thrives instead of places where death thrives. There is life in the commandments (Lu 10:28) and death in sin (Rom 6:23). All God has said to us in the OT and the NT is to the end that we avoid the ways of death and choose the ways of life.

"My little children, these things I write to you, so that you may not sin. And if anyone sins, we have an Advocate with the Father, Jesus Christ the righteous." 1 John 2:1 (NKJV).

11-5
An Army Of Lambs
The seventy were commissioned to go out and announce the Kingdom of God. Jesus said to them, "Go; behold, I send you out as lambs in the midst of wolves" (Luke 10:3, NASB). Crazy? Off the charts crazy! Counterintuitive? You bet! The Jesus way? Absolutely! Sometimes lambs convert wolves to become lambs. Sometimes lambs can only show wolves how lambs die. Sometimes the persecuting wolf sees it, turns to the Lamb of God and joins the army of the lambs. The death of Stephen-- the lamb, pricked the heart of Saul--the wolf!

11-6
The Beheading Of Paul
Paul was a great persecutor of the church. He said in his testimony, "I persecuted this Way to the death, binding and putting both men and women into prisons" Acts 22:4 (NASB). After his conversion to Christianity, he was shown by Jesus, "How much he

must suffer for My name's sake" Acts 9:16 (NASB). And suffer he did (2 Cor 11:22-28)! In the end, Paul was beheaded. Absent from the body, he was present with his Lord (2 Cor 5:8). He would proclaim Jesus being the promised Messiah, no matter the price! May it be so with us!

"Indeed, all who desire to live godly in Christ Jesus will be persecuted. But evil men and impostors will proceed from bad to worse, deceiving and being deceived." 2 Timothy 3:12-13 (NASB)

11-7
Kingdom Visions

William McCants' new book, *The ISIS Apocalypse,* shows that through radical beheadings and crucifixions, Isis believes they are preparing the way for the end of the world and the arrival of the Kingdom of God. Christians believe that the Kingdom has arrived in Jesus the Messiah and will come fully when He returns to this earth. Jesus rejected violence to establish His peaceful kingdom, rather choosing deeds of compassion to advance the work of God. ISIS seeks to establish it by violence. Two different visions! Two different theologies! We cannot force the Kingdom of God by our actions; we surrender to its presence by surrendering to Messiah, King of Kingdom of God and using the methods He did.

"As you go, proclaim the good news, 'The kingdom of heaven has come near.' Cure the sick, raise the dead, cleanse the lepers, cast out demons." Matthew 10:7-8a (NRSV)

11-8
Responding Words
Our reactions are as important as our actions. If someone speaks a hurtful word to us, we are to speak a healing word to them. Jesus taught us that we are to respond to curses with blessings. Harsh words need kind responses. If people are having a bad day, and say something they will regret later, do not add to it by making a bad day for yourself. This is not easy. It requires patience and grace. It requires self-discipline. The Lord of grace will help us to show grace in our reactions.

"Bless those who curse you, pray for those who mistreat you." Luke 6:28 (NASB)

11-9
The Infinite Mind
Our mind need not stand isolated. One of the things that we need to realize is that our mind is connected to the Infinite Mind. Our rationality is an expression of that Mind. Our mind can be in touch with His Mind. We need its communication. The history of Biblical revelation is that this Infinite Mind has chosen to make Himself known to us. The sum of that revelation is Jesus of Nazareth, who is made to us "wisdom from God" (I Cor 1:30). In Him God still speaks!

"For who has known the mind of the Lord so as to instruct him? But we have the mind of Christ." 1 Corinthians 2:16 (NRSV)

11-10
Usual And Unusual
Our devotional and worship times have their routines and their rituals. This is the way of developing good habits. Sometimes the routine is interrupted with a surprising sense of joy when the fountain of the Spirit overflows. That does not happen every day, nor should we expect it. But the regular times give structure and opportunity for unusual worship moments. Some people are cued only for the unusual and miss the strength and character that daily routine can give.

"See, I have longed for your precepts; in your righteousness give me life. Let your steadfast love come to me, O LORD, your salvation according to your promise." Psalm 119:40-41 (NRSV)

11-11
Old Time Prophets
The Pharisees carefully built elaborate markers for the graves of the martyred prophets. Their nostalgia was saying, "Those were the great days of powerful words from the Lord." Yet, they despised the prophetic words of John the Baptist and Jesus. In fact, they wanted no present word from the Lord to confront their sin. Paul would say later, "Do not despise the words of prophets" (1 Thess 5:20 NRSV). We still do not like words that confront our immorality, racism, sexism, nationalism, materialism, hedonism, apathy and other sins. We choose rather to remember the great non-threatening days of yore!

"Woe to you! For you build the tombs of the prophets, and it was your fathers who killed them. So you are witnesses and approve the deeds of your fathers; because it was they who killed them, and you build their tombs." Luke 11:47-48 (NASB)

11-12
Openness And Timing

There are times in our lives when we cannot even hear the things we need to hear. *Where we are* causes us to miss it. We all can remember that there were things out there that we could have heard and should have heard, but because of immaturity, did not. We cannot change that, but can learn from it. With honest self-knowledge, openness to truth, and with the grace of the Holy Spirit we can profit greatly from new light and grow spiritually.

Dear Lord, work in my heart to expose those places in me that prevent me from hearing what You want so much for me to hear. You desire that I grow in an unhindered way. Help me to not be that hindrance. Amen!

11-13
Unity Among God's People

Jesus taught us to work out our differences face to face (Matt 18:15). When we have grievances with a sister or brother, we are to go to them and not a third party. It is too easy to talk to others to make our one-sided case. This has a divisive effect. We are not to talk *about* each other but talk *to* each other. We are members of a common family who relate to each other as brothers and sisters. Our spiritual growth has lots to do with how we relate to others.

"All of you, have unity of spirit, sympathy, love for one another, a tender heart, and a humble mind" 1 Peter 3:8 (NRSV).

11-14
Many Surrenders

There are critical surrenders in our life that are pivotal and life changing. But all of these surrenders become a pattern for a lifestyle of surrender. The initial surrender is tested and lived out in a lifetime of daily surrenders. We enter more than one door marked "surrender". This certainly does not mean that each following surrender is to be a battle ground. But it does mean that we live out, in fidelity and faithfulness, our earlier once-for-all vows to the Lord in ongoing daily choices.

Father, I have surrendered and do surrender my life with all of its twists and turns to you. I completely give you myself, and desire always to live that gift out in all the tests that will come. By your grace, enable me to carry out this intent. In Jesus' Holy Name I pray.

11-15
Dwelling On The Past

Recreating a past event may be a good thing to establish justice in a court of law, but it can be a poor thing in our personal lives. We cannot go back and relive, redo or repair the past. Once it is past, we cannot fix the accident, stop the divorce, regain the lost opportunity, reverse the storm, etc. We are where we are, and so we have to begin here. Do not keep trying to relive what you cannot undo. Live each day relying on the Lord, so that today may not become tomorrow's regret.

"My heart has no desire to stay
Where doubts arise
And fears dismay.
Tho' some may dwell where these abound,
My prayer, my aim, is higher ground."   -Johnson Oatman, Jr.

11-16
Standing Right

We have confused *standing for the right* as criticizing everyone who does not see things as we do. *Standing for right* is also an attitude that we express. We stand for *right* in the Spirit of Christ. We can speak right truth with a wrong attitude and still be wrong. We are told that we are to speak the truth in love. This is standing for truth with the attitude of Christ.

"Instead, speaking the truth in love, we will in all things grow up into him who is the Head, that is, Christ. From him the whole body, joined and held together by every supporting ligament, grows and builds itself up in love, as each part does its work." Ephesians 4:15-16 (NIV)

11-17
Answered In Time

The answers to many of life's questions do not come in immediate answers but in years of living. Some answers cannot be discovered until we live them. Even then, we will not have all the answers. We do

184

not need to have all the answers to do the right thing and to be faithful. Carry with you a little bag marked *unanswered questions.* Put your questions there. Keep serving God and you will be surprised, over time, how many things will come out of your bag *answered.*

"These things His disciples did not understand at the first; but when Jesus was glorified, then they remembered that these things were written of Him, and that they had done these things to Him." John 12:16 (NASB)

11-18
Losses And Gains
Learning to live with your losses is as important as learning to live with your successes. We had a hand full of sand and the tide washed it away. Our carefully constructed castles were lapped up by life's waves. We had hopes that were devastated and dreams that did not come to pass. We made plans that were changed by another's choices. How we deal with these things is important. It can build fortitude, determination and character. It can rearrange our priorities and get the fluff out of our lives. In this way our losses become gains.

"Now I'm glad—not that you were upset, but that you were jarred into turning things around. You let the distress bring you to God, not drive you from him. The result was all gain, no loss." 2 Corinthians 7:9 (The Message)

11-19
The Spirit Of The Shepherd
When you are lost you can get lots of bad advice. People who have never been there will tell you how to go. Some will tell you where you are, and their total misunderstanding will hurt your feelings. You need someone who truly knows you to give you direction. More than that, you need someone who truly loves you and really cares about what will happen to you in the end. You need the Shepherd, the very Spirit of the Shepherd living inside of you. He will guide you into "all the truth" (Jn 16:13). He brings you truth about yourself that you did not know. He brings you truth about God on which you can act.

11-20
Grateful For The Earth
Most people are several steps removed from the growing plants that feed us and are necessary for our survival. We are distant from a fruit bearing earth and those who tend it. Without someone to plant, tend and gather, where would we be? More than that, without God's earth, sun and rain, where would we be? The rich variety of food that God has provided us in the earth staggers the imagination. When the earth feeds us we should be grateful to the Creator.

"Let the peoples praise You, O God; Let all the peoples praise You. The earth has yielded its produce; God, our God, blesses us. God blesses us, that all the ends of the earth may fear Him." Psalm 67:5-7 (NASB)

11-21
Thankful For His Plans
So many things in my life have come to me in spite of my planning, and even contrary to my dreams. Out of the ashes of failed dreams and unrealized plans has come a garden of richness. Flowers are blooming. Fruit is coming. It is impossible for me to take credit because it was not what I had planned. So here I sit in humble gratitude for the faithful providences of my Father.

Father, thank You for changing my plans. Thank You for closing that door that I wanted so much to walk through. Thank You for not giving me all the things for which I asked. Thank You for using Your wisdom when I was begging for You to use Your power. Thank You for the discipline that seemed so hard at the time. Now I see grace in all of these changed plans. Amen!

11-22
It Is A Blessing
Everything that brings you to genuine humility, everything that brings you down from your self-importance, everything that strips you of self-sufficiency, everything that discomforts your kingdom compliancy, everything that brings you from your strident walk to your knees, every crisis that turns your eyes toward Jesus, every problem that makes you look to the Lord, all these things are for you a blessing.

"Is there yet any seed left in the barn? Until now, the vine and the fig tree, the pomegranate and the olive tree have not borne fruit. "'From this day on I will bless you.'" Haggai 2:19 (NIV)

11-23
Gratitude And Forgiveness

The Father's forgiveness of us is greater than our forgiveness of others. His is greater because our offenses against the Father are the greater crimes. His forgiveness is greater because of His justice. It is greater because our sin is so opposite His holiness. If the Father has so forgiven us of our trespasses against Him, we can do no other than forgive His other children's trespasses against us. To not forgive is the height of ingratitude to our Father's forgiveness of us.

"In him we have redemption through his blood, the forgiveness of our trespasses, according to the riches of his grace." Ephesians 1:7 (NRSV)

11-24
Grateful For The Invisible

It seems that we thank God most for the tangibles we can see and hold in our hands. We hold all this stuff in our hands and say, "I am blessed." But what about the unseen intangibles? The spiritual world! The heavenly things! Silent guarding angels! Undetected providences! The gifts of the Spirit! The fruit of the Spirit! Heavenly manna! The well springing up in our hearts! The invisible God sustains us with His invisible things that flow from Him to us.

188

"By faith he (Moses) forsook Egypt, not fearing the wrath of the king: for he endured, as seeing him who is invisible." Hebrews 11:27 (KJV)

11-25
Gratefully Give Blessings

We frequently say, "I am blessed" or "God has been good to me." Indeed it is true! God has been good to us so we will be good to each other. God has blessed us so we can bless others. A good job is so that we will have something to give. A good day is so we can enable another to have a good day. If goodness stops with us then it will decay our souls. If we give it away we will find we still have it. If, in gratitude, we share our blessings we will be twice blessed.

"Let him who stole steal no longer, but rather let him labor, working with his hands what is good, that he may have something to give him who has need." Ephesians 4:28 (NKJV)

11-26
Grateful For The Son Of God

Our gratitude should overflow for the Son of God. He came from the Father and perfectly shows us the Father. Because of Him, we can say that God is love. By Him, we can relate to God as Father. He accepts prodigals and aliens into the family of God. We were far off, and He brought us near (Eph 2:13). We were outside, and He let us in. In Him, the rejected are accepted. In Him, the lost are found. He sets captives free. He brings the poor into heavenly riches. This Great Gift drives us to gratitude and worship.

"And the angel answered and said unto her, The Holy Ghost shall come upon thee, and the power of the Highest shall overshadow thee: therefore also that holy thing which shall be born of thee shall be called the Son of God." Luke 1:35 (KJV)

11-27
Captured By Gratitude

I am not sure that I know how to explain this, but there have been moments in my life when I have been captured by gratitude. It is like it just comes and takes me away. Oddly enough, it can come in sad times when grief wants to run out of my eyes, but gratitude carries me along as my happy companion. Joy and sorrow, grief and gratitude have sung to me. Gratitude carried the melody and I worshiped. It is a mystery! How can I feel gratitude in the midst of pain and sorrow? Yet, I do! When gratitude comes, I find joy in having been made the captive of a good and generous God.

"I bow down toward your holy temple and give thanks to your name for your steadfast love and your faithfulness, for you have exalted above all things your name and your word." Psalm 138:2 (ESV)

11-28
A Gratitude Spring

Real thanksgiving begins as gratitude in the mind and heart. Gratitude is the spring, and thanksgiving is the overflow. When there is gratitude in the heart, music will arise. It wells up as songs of praise. Gratitude washes our eyes and changes how we see our circumstances. Our story changes for the better when gratitude flows into our narrative. When it flows out of our well, the water tastes better to us and to others who drink from our well.

"I will give thanks to You, O Lord my God, with all my heart, and will glorify Your name forever." Psalm 86:12 (NASB)

11-29
Debt Of Gratitude
Every stream we ride flows in a channel prepared by water that went before it. Some of these waters have persistently cut their way through rocks. So much of the wisdom and ways we have learned, we owe to rich traditions that went before us. Knowledge did not start with us. We have walked in paths marked out by other feet. We pick fruit from trees planted by others. We drink water from wells dug by others. In our arrogance and self-sufficiency, we need to know this debt we owe; not just know it, but be grateful for it.

"Now I praise you because you remember me in everything and hold firmly to the traditions, just as I delivered them to you." 1 Corinthians 11:2 (NASB)

11-30
God Loves The World
God chose, in His magnificent mercy and super-abounding love, to enter the stream of human history as a human. He did not abandon His creation, but came to it. He not only came to it, He came fully into it. The Creator became the creature. "He was in the world and the world was made by Him and the world

did not know him" (Jn 1:10). Because "God so loved the world", Jesus was given to the world. He did not come to pour out condemnation on it (Jn 3:16), for He will eventually restore the world into new creation. He is, even now, making kingdom citizens ready for it.

12-1
The Bible And The Word

"In the beginning was the Word, and the Word was with God, and the Word was God" John 1:1 (KJV). "Long ago, at many times and in many ways, God spoke to our fathers by the prophets, but in these last days he has spoken to us by his Son" Hebrews 1:1-2a (ESV). God's final authoritative Word is a person named Jesus of Nazareth. He embodies all that God wants to say to us. His teachings and person fills up with new meanings all the old writings. The purpose of the Bible is to faithfully reveal to us Christ, the infallible Word. The Bible, through the Spirit of the Word, faithfully reveals Him to us. We study the Bible to study Jesus.

12-2
Jesus Reveals God

Jesus stooped to the weakness of humanity who had lost the ability to see God as He really is. Messiah came as the revelation of God. The Roman centurion, who witnessed the crucifixion, said, "Surely this was the Son of God." The person, teachings and actions of Jesus radiated God. In Him, we see a God of love in quest of us. In Him, we find acceptance in the place of condemnation. In Him, the glory of the wilderness tabernacle has come down in Jesus Messiah, our Temple.

"And He is the radiance of His glory and the exact representation of His nature" Hebrews 1:3a (NASB)

12-3
Creator And Savior

John said of the Word, "All things were made by him; and without him was not anything made that was made" John 1:3 (KJV). The writer of Hebrews also says, "Through whom also he created the world...he upholds the universe by the word of his power. After making purification for sins, he sat down at the right hand of the Majesty on high" Hebrews 1:2-3 (ESV). It took the Creator to save us. An angel could not do it. We, along with the earth, are fallen, but the Savior has come, is here, and will come, all for this great rescue. The Saving Creator is our hope.

12-4
The Divine Imprint

"He is the radiance of the glory of God and the exact imprint of his nature" Hebrews 1:3 (ESV). Through Christ, we have become partakers of the divine nature (2 Peter 1:4). We are to be conformed to His image. (Rom 8:29). We are being changed into His likeness (2 Cor 3:18). The more we look at Jesus, the more we live with Him, the more we walk with Him, the more He is imprinted on us, the more He is restoring us to His image, and thus to the likeness of God.

"O to be like Thee, blessed Redeemer- this is my constant longing and prayer.

"Gladly I'll forfeit all of earth's treasures, Jesus, Thy perfect likeness to wear.

"O to be like Thee! O to be like Thee, Blessed Redeemer, pure as Thou art!

"Come in Thy sweetness; come in Thy fullness.

"Stamp Thine own image deep on my heart." -Thomas O. Chisholm

12-5
King Of Angels

The shepherds heard the announcement of King Jesus from angels. The angels point to One who is superior to them. "Having become as much superior to angels as the name he has inherited is more excellent than theirs" Hebrews 1:4 (ESV). The Son of God is Lord over the angels, but became lower than angels in order to liberate the world from the forces of sin and death. By His own death, He defeated our true enemies. He is now putting all things under His feet. Angels, and all creation, bow before the Triumphant Son.

"For it was not to angels that God subjected the world to come, of which we are speaking. It has been testified somewhere, 'What is man, that you are mindful of him, or the son of man, that you care for him? You made him for a little while lower than the angels; you have crowned him with glory and honor, putting everything in subjection under his feet.' Now in putting everything in subjection to him, he left nothing outside his control. At present, we do not yet see everything in subjection to him. But we see him who for a little while was made lower than the angels, namely Jesus, crowned with glory and honor because of the suffering of death, so that by the grace of God he might taste death for everyone." Hebrews 2:5-9 (ESV)

12-6
Exalted King And Priest

For the Son to return to the Father's right hand was to vindicate His priestly sacrifice and to affirm that He still rules the Kingdom of God. "After making purification for sins, he sat down at the right hand of the Majesty on high" (Heb 1:3b ESV). When He ascended into Heaven, it was not to withdraw from His kingdom, but to be enthroned over it. He is there to rule until all enemies are put under His feet. As Priest, He is there in solidarity with humanity, in His resurrected body, to intercede for us. He who is one with the Father, is one with us, and is our real atonement (*at-one-ment*). His intercession joins God and humans in His own glorified flesh.

12-7
Gentle King

In the ancient world, Kings governed by brutality and the abuse of power. They ruled by fear and intimidation. Jesus came as the Gentle King whose methods were kindness, grace and love. This Gentle King was approachable. Sinners wanted to draw near (Lu 15:1). He had not come to condemn. He came to rescue. His weapon was love. Jesus' love creates an atmosphere where communities and individuals can blossom. As He has embraced them, His kingdom citizens live to embrace others. His gentle subjects will inherit the earth. (Matt 5:5).

"Take My yoke upon you and learn from Me, for I am gentle and lowly in heart, and you will find rest for your souls." Matthew 11:29 (NKJV)

12-8
Humble King

Our King is humble. The Humble One was born in a stable and laid in a manger. He grew up in a peasant family. His triumphant entry was on a donkey. He humbly awaits admission to anyone who will open the door (Rev 3:20). He came incognito into the world He made (Jn 1:10). Moses was humble (Nu 12:3), but Jesus embodied humility. His Kingdom citizens have rejected exalting themselves and chosen the path of humility. How can we walk in pride in the face of our Humble King?

"Rejoice greatly, O daughter of Zion! Shout in triumph, O daughter of Jerusalem! Behold, your king is coming to you; He is just and endowed with salvation, Humble, and mounted on a donkey, Even on a colt, the foal of a donkey." Zechariah 9:9 (NASB)

12-9
King Of Bread

The world wants kings that will give them bread aplenty. Jesus multiplied bread to feed thousands. His kingdom citizens are commanded to feed the hungry. It is no accident that the King of Bread was placed in a manger (feeding trough). He is the true Manna from Heaven that gives life to the world. We are all starving paupers who have found this Bread and are delighted to invite one and all to come to the table with us. We go out and find them anywhere we can, because He wants His house filled with guests (Lu 14:23).

"For the bread of God is He who comes down from heaven and gives life to the world." Then they said to Him, "Lord, give us this bread always." And Jesus said to them, "I am the bread of life. He who comes to Me shall never hunger, and he who believes in Me shall never thirst." John 6:33-35 (NKJV)

12-10
Warrior King

Our Warrior King has set Himself against the evil powers of darkness. He cast out demonic powers by the *finger of God*, demonstrating the arrival of His kingdom (Lu 11:20). He has come to defeat our old enemies of sin and death. He will not stop until He has put all enemies under His feet (I Cor 15:25). The cross and resurrection declare Messiah is Victor. As citizens of His kingdom we are armed to take back territory from the evil one and hand it over to our King.

"And she gave birth to a son, a male child, who is to rule all the nations with a rod of iron; and her child was caught up to God and to His throne." Revelation 12:5 (NASB)

12-11
King Of Love

Our King of Love was a gift of the Father's love (Jn 3:16). His offering of Himself was love's sweet smelling aroma (Eph 5:2). The love of Messiah surpasses knowledge (Eph 3:19). Nothing can separate us from Messiah's love (Rom 8:35). His

Kingdom citizens are identified by loving God with their whole being and their neighbor as themselves (Lu 10:27). To love this way is His royal law (Jas 2:8). His weapon of love is still the most powerful weapon for taking the world. Use no other weapons in love's place.

"But God commended his love toward us, in that, while we were yet sinners, Messiah (King) died for us." (Rom 5:8)

12-12
King Of Peace
Jesus is called the Prince of Peace (Isa 9:6). He creates peace between God and humans (Rom 5:1), and when He is obeyed, between humans and humans. His kingdom citizens are peacemakers, and thus are children of God (Matt 5:9). He does not rule by totalitarian control, or forced submission, and call it peace. He does not crucify nor behead to establish His rule in the world. Instead, He was crucified for all humans. The King of Peace does not force His kingdom by terrorism and violence, but took upon himself the terror of the Romans in order to establish His peace. The subjects of the King of Peace are people of peace!

"And let the peace of God rule in your hearts, to which also you were called in one body; and be thankful." Colossians 3:15 (NKJV)

12-13
King Of Light
Jesus is the Light of the World. As Christians we "share in the inheritance of the saints in the kingdom of light" Col 1:12b (NIV). Jesus is King of the Kingdom of Light. He who was Light said, "Let there be light". The darkness cannot overcome this Light (Jn 1:5). To walk in His light is to have fellowship with God and forgiveness of sins (I Jn 1:7). Kingdom citizens walk as "children of light" (Eph 5:8). If they claim to know this Light and still walk in sin's darkness they are deceived (I Jn 1:6). The King of Light has made His kingdom citizens His light bearers (Mt 5:14-16).

Then Jesus again spoke to them, saying, "I am the Light of the world; he who follows Me will not walk in the darkness, but will have the Light of life." John 8:12 (NASB)

12-14
Shepherd King
David was a shepherd king. So was Jesus. The OT called kings shepherds. Their duty was not to serve themselves but the people. If they did not, they were under God's judgment (Ezk 34:1-20). The king was to stand up for the widow, orphan and the other disenfranchised ones. Kings were to see to it that there was justice for all in the kingdom, preventing the rich from taking advantage of the poor. Kings were to create economic situations where all had bread. The Kingdom of God has a Shepherd King. The citizens of the Kingdom share His mission of meeting people's needs.

"And I will set up one shepherd over them, and he shall feed them, even my servant David; he shall feed them, and he shall be their shepherd." Ezekiel 34:23 (KJV)

12-15
King Of Grace
Our Messiah King is the King of Grace. He is the great gift of grace, in His own person, demonstrated by His incarnation. He is the giver of grace, not as mere unmerited favor, but as "grace to help in the time of need" (Heb 14:16). He mediates and embodies the grace of His Father and our Father. The King of Grace gives us His Spirit. His Spirit is called *the Spirit of grace* (Heb 10:29). The law was given by Moses, but grace and truth came by Messiah (Jn 1:17). By His grace we are rescued (Ac 15:11). His kingdom citizens give His grace as freely as they have received it.

"The grace of our Lord Jesus Messiah be with you all." Amen (Rom 16:24).

12-16
Merciful King
"Grace, mercy, and peace (are) from God the Father and the Lord Jesus Messiah our Savior" (Titus 1:4). Mercy flows to us from the Father through King Jesus. His great mercy has given us a living hope (I Pet 1:3). Without mercy we would be without hope. In Him, mercy triumphs over justice and grace over law. We pray, "Lord Jesus Christ, Son of God, have mercy on me and rescue me!" The sure sign that we as kingdom citizens have truly received God's mercy is

that we give it.   It is impossible to understand the cross and do otherwise. The merciful will obtain mercy (Matt 5:7).

"Keep yourselves in God's love as you wait for the mercy of our Lord Jesus Christ to bring you to eternal life." Jude 1:21 (NIV)

12-17
The King Who Judges
Our Messiah King is coming to judge the living and the dead (2 Tim 4:1). "God will judge the secrets of men through Messiah Jesus" (Rom 2:16).   His love does not soften His ability to judge.   He will judge between sheep and goats, between the genuine and hypocrite, alloy and gold, and between saint and sinner. At the judgment, the compassionate Christ will judge those who showed no compassion.   His love will judge those who chose not to love.   All will be judged for their own actions by the One who came and modeled right actions.

"Before the LORD, for He is coming to judge the earth; He will judge the world with righteousness and the peoples with equity." Psalm 98:9 (NASB)

12-18
Servant King
"I did not come to be served but to serve" (Mt 20:28). He served with a towel and basin.   He served by healing the sick and casting out demons. He served by teaching the Scriptures. He served by feeding the hungry and lifting up the poor.   He served by the broken bread and the shared cup. His kingdom is a

kingdom of servants, citizens who give themselves away for others. They do not come to sit at the top being served, but they delight in going to the bottom in order to serve others.

"For who is greater, the one who reclines at the table or the one who serves? Is it not the one who reclines at the table? But I am among you as the one who serves." Luke 22:27 (NASB)

12-19
Suffering King

Jesus Messiah was Isaiah's Suffering Servant. He who embodied Israel suffered as Israel's representative. The rabbis of Israel never joined the idea of Messiah and the Suffering Servant being one and the same person. Jesus did (Lu 24:26). Peter, reflecting the theology of the day, was rebuked for trying to turn Jesus from his announced path of suffering (Mt 16:23). The merging of these two biblical themes into one Person reveals God's great plan of redemption. Jesus chose to rescue through suffering. His kingdom citizens are to count it joy to suffer with Him (Mt 5:11-12).

"Surely our griefs He Himself bore, And our sorrows He carried; yet we ourselves esteemed Him stricken, Smitten of God, and afflicted. But He was pierced through for our transgressions, He was crushed for our iniquities; the chastening for our well-being fell upon Him, and by His scourging we are healed. All of us like sheep have gone astray, each of us has turned to his own way; but the LORD has caused the iniquity of us all to fall on Him." Isaiah 53:4-6 (NASB)

12-20
The King With Good News
"Repent for the Kingdom of Heaven is at hand" is coupled with good news. The kingdom of God has arrived with King Jesus. The good news, or *gospel of the kingdom*, is that Jesus is God's promised Messiah sent to establish the Kingdom of God. Good news has been made to serve the evangelical view of personal salvation. It is that, but it is much bigger than that. The good news is that the Kingdom of God has been brought near by Jesus and that the King of the Jews is also Lord of the Gentiles and the whole earth. He will not stop until His Kingdom has come, and His will is done on earth, as it is in heaven.

"Now after John was put in prison, Jesus came to Galilee, preaching the gospel of the kingdom of God, and saying, "The time is fulfilled, and the kingdom of God is at hand. Repent, and believe in the good news." Mark 1:14-15

12-21
King Of The Whole Earth
He who was first acclaimed *King of the Jews* is in conquest of the whole earth. "The LORD has said to Me, 'You are My Son, Today I have begotten You. Ask of Me, and I will give You The nations for Your inheritance, and the ends of the earth for Your possession" (Psalm 2:7-8 NKJV). No national or provincial king will save the world. Only the Lord of Heaven and earth can do that. The earth, now divided by language, culture and geography, will one day be reunited under the Father's Son. We worship Him now anticipating that glorious restoration of all creation.

12-22
Faithful King
God has made a covenant with us. He is faithful to that covenant. "For the word of the LORD is upright, and all His work is done in faithfulness" (Psalm 33:4 NASB). His covenant with us is the New Covenant sealed with the blood of the cross (Mt 26:28). We hold our faith in His promises, in full confidence, without wavering, for we know "He is faithful that promised" (Heb 10:23). Our Faithful King is reliable. The one life that God has given you, trust it completely to him.

"Know therefore that the LORD your God, He is God, the faithful God, who keeps His covenant and His lovingkindness to a thousandth generation with those who love Him and keep His commandments." Deuteronomy 7:9 (NASB)

12-23
Righteous King
The kings of old who brought about fairness and justice in their kingdoms were called righteous. When the right was not present, the people longed for a king who would rescue (save) them from unrighteousness and reestablish equity in the kingdom. Jesus is that rescuing king (Zec 9:9). "Great and marvelous are Your works, O Lord God, the Almighty; Righteous and true are Your ways, King of the nations!" (Rev 15:3b NASB). We worship our king by doing righteousness (Isa 58:6-7).

"Behold, the days come, saith the LORD, that I will raise unto David a righteous Branch, and a King shall reign and prosper, and shall execute judgment and justice in the earth." Jeremiah 23:5 (KJV)

12-24
Son Of David

The Messiah came as a descendant of King David and His kingdom will not come to an end (Isa 9:7). He would come as the Shoot from the stem of Jesse (Isa 11:1). He would be born in David's town of Bethlehem (Lu 2:4). This Son of David is the Lord of David. He was before David. One day David, with all creation, will bow before Him. This Son of David brings the Kingdom of God to all who will come under His rule. "Have mercy on us, Son of David!" (Matt 9:27).

"He shall be great, and shall be called the Son of the Highest: and the Lord God shall give unto him the throne of his father David: And he shall reign over the house of Jacob forever; and of his kingdom there shall be no end." Luke 1:32-33 (KJV)

12-25
Saving King

"For unto you is born this day in the city of David a Savior, which is Messiah the Lord" (Luke 2:11). Savior means one who rescues or delivers. This One who rescues is the long promised Messiah, the hope of all nations. He has come to rescue us from our captivity to sin and to set us free. He has come to rescue by His good governance. His intention is to establish His kind of government in the face of the corrupt governments of the nations. His Kingdom is the only hope of this world.

12-26
King Of The Jews

The wise men came enquiring, "Where is he who is born King of the Jews" (Mt 2:2). Herod sought to kill Him because of the title. Pilate asked Him if He was the "King of the Jews" (Mt 27:11). The title was used to mock Him (Mt 27:29). It was placed as a placard over the cross (Mt 27:37). The coming of the Gentile Magi recognized His kingship and foresaw the time when every knee will bow and every ethnic tongue will confess (Rom 14:11) this King of the Jews as their King also. Peace on earth!

12-27
Terrorism In Bethlehem

Innocent boy babies were wiped out of Bethlehem by Herod's brutal Roman forces. Mothers sobbed! The boy Jesus escaped, but only for a few years. He would return to a vocation of suffering and submit to a Roman death. Though the Roman cross was a tool of terror, Jesus turned it into an altar for sacrifice. Jesus embraced suffering, knowing that love would triumph over hate. It did! It still does! The terrorists did not win! The crucified Messiah did!

"A voice was heard in Ramah, wailing and loud lamentation, Rachel weeping for her children; she refused to be consoled, because they are no more." Matthew 2:18 (NRSV)

12-28
Coming King

A cloud received the ascending Jesus out of the sight of His upward gazing followers (Acts 1). That mysterious cloud will some day open itself to reveal the descending Christ. His servants are "waiting for the coming of our Lord Jesus Messiah" (1 Cor 1:7). His sanctifying work prepares His kingdom citizens to be "without blame" at His coming (I Thess 3:13, 5:23). He is coming "with all His saints" (I Thess 3:13). The Lord's Prayer will be fulfilled. The Kingdom will come fully and finally when the King returns.

"He who testifies to these things says, "Surely I am coming quickly." Amen. Even so, come, Lord Jesus! The grace of our Lord Jesus Christ be with you all. Amen." Revelation 22:20-21 (NKJV)

12-29
Reigning King
Jesus is Lord! He arose from the dead as Victor! He ascended to the right hand of His Father! He sits enthroned over all kings, governors, presidents and rulers as their Ruler and Lord. He is the King over kings and the Lord over lords. He who reigns above is working His will below by those who pray, "Thy kingdom come, Thy will be done on earth as in Heaven." His Kingdom citizens will come to life and reign with Him (Rev 20:4). Glorious day!

"And the seventh angel sounded; and there were great voices in heaven, saying, The kingdoms of this world are become the kingdoms of our Lord, and of his Christ; and he shall reign for ever and ever." Revelation 11:15 (KJV)

12-30
Worthy King

Jesus is worthy because God has exalted Him and "given Him a name which is above every name" (Phil 2:9). He is worthy because He lived out the vocation given to Him by His Father. He is worthy because of His holiness. He is worthy because of His sacrificial death as the Lamb of God. He is worthy because He cares for the sheep. He does not rule as one hungry for power and vain glory. He humbly seeks the glory of His Father. He actively seeks the good of the governed. He alone is worthy!

"Saying with a loud voice, worthy is the Lamb that was slain to receive power, and riches, and wisdom, and strength, and honor, and glory, and blessing." Revelation 5:12 (KJV)

12-31
Making The Most Of Your Time

Time moves rapidly. An old year comes to an end and a new year begins. One era of our lives fades into a new one. How we use our time is a part of our stewardship. Time gone cannot be recovered. The way we use our time is the way we build our lives. Invest the moment in serving Christ and others. Be present in real time with those you love. In this way we redeem time and make the most of every opportunity.

"Therefore be careful how you walk, not as unwise men but as wise, making the most of your time, because the days are evil." Ephesians 5:15-16 (NASB)

Benediction

"Now may the God of hope fill you with all joy and peace in believing, so that you will abound in hope by the power of the Holy Spirit." Romans 15:13 (NASB)

65138699R00116

Made in the USA
Charleston, SC
11 December 2016